# BEFORE THEIR TIME

# BEFORE
# THEIR
# TIME

A Memoir

*Robert Kotlowitz*

Alfred A. Knopf   New York   1998

THIS IS A BORZOI BOOK
PUBLISHED BY ALFRED A. KNOPF, INC.

http://www.randomhouse.com/

Chapter 3 is adapted from "Bliss It Was" by
Robert Kotlowitz, which appeared in *The New York Times
Magazine,* May 7, 1995.

Grateful acknowledgment is made to Sussman & Associates
on behalf of Donaldson Publishing Company, and The
Songwriters Guild of America on behalf of Gilbert Keyes
Music Company, for permission to reprint an excerpt from
"My Buddy" by Walter Donaldson and Gus Kahn, copyright © 1922,
copyright renewed 1949. International copyright secured.
All rights reserved. Used by permission.

Library of Congress Cataloging-in-Publication Data
Kotlowitz, Robert.
Before their time : a memoir / by Robert Kotlowitz.
p.   cm.
ISBN 0-679-44789-X
1. Kotlowitz, Robert.   2. World War, 1939–1945—
Personal narratives, American.   3. United States.
Army—Biography.   4. Soldiers—United States—
Biography.   I. Title.
D811.K647   1997
940.54'8173—dc20      96-26700      CIP

Manufactured in the United States of America
Published February 3, 1998
Reprinted Twice
Fourth Printing, August 1998

*To my sons, Dan and Alex, and their families*

# CONTENTS

BEFORE THEIR TIME

# My Buddies

IN 1943, I was a pre-med day student at Johns Hopkins University, in Baltimore, Maryland. Half the student body at Hopkins during World War II was pre-med; it was a respectable way of evading the draft. But I was a fraud on campus, and not the only one. I didn't want to be a doctor. I had no interest in medicine, or in science of any kind. And so, even though I was a smart kid, my school marks showed mostly C's and D's and enough F's to put me on probation. At eighteen, which was how old I was then, this record almost paralyzed me. I knew in my bones that I was going to flunk out and that there was nothing I could do about it. Maybe I even wanted to flunk out.

The Army soon intervened. With my lousy marks, they drafted me right out of the classroom. I was there one day, gone the next. Naturally, I rationalized the process, to soothe my pride. I told myself that it was better than being blatantly tossed out of college, for all the world to see and judge, better than being humiliated at home, where my embarrassed parents had grown used to a near-lifetime of straight A's as I made my way through the Baltimore public schools. And besides, I believed in the war. It seemed just and righteous to me. In my simpleminded, adolescent way, I hated the Nazis. I knew that terrible things were happening everywhere. I understood perfectly well, however many courses I may have failed, that I was living in a murderous century, one without pity and probably without precedent.

I was ready to go.

On the morning I left my suburban home for the Army, my family gathered on the front porch to say good-bye. Mother, father, kid sister, aligned in a row; and I facing them, hungry to be off. We were all almost unbearably self-conscious. My father, I remember, hesitantly covered his eyes with one hand, unable to look at me—a strange and powerful gesture that stays with me to this day. My mother stood rigidly still, her lips thin, suffering in silence. Poor beleaguered parents, ever stoic. Alongside my mother, my sister, who was almost seven years younger than I, stared up at me, worshipping her hero through allergy-swollen eyes.

I danced around in excruciating pain for a couple of seconds in front of them, mumbled a few words of farewell, and, in another moment, was gone.

FOURTEEN months later, in October of 1944, I was stationed on the outskirts of the city of Nancy, in France, in a dilapidated old Alsatian warehouse that was filled with hungry rats and pools of dirty rainwater. I was on guard duty at the time—an ignoble occupation chosen for me by my superiors—keeping an eye on the duffel bags that belonged to the infantrymen of the 26th Division. (I had recently been one of those infantrymen myself.) The 26th was then at the front, several miles away, where it had replaced the Fourth Armored Division in the Fourth's old dug-in positions.

I shared the warehouse with three other GIs, all of whom were strangers to me. Together we slept on a filthy straw pallet that was stretched across the floor of what was once a receiving room. The straw smelled of urine and cow dung and we smelled of soiled underwear; a pungent crew, trapped in each other's sweaty company. To keep warm, we burned sooty coal in an antique stove that threatened our mattress with flying sparks whenever it flared up. We were always putting out small fires in the middle of the night, cursing the stove and the warehouse and the indifference of fate in general. None of us had ever lived this way before.

We survived. We had heat, food, and shelter, everything that was needed for a bitter winter to come, including the long woolen underwear that hung on us like potato sacks. But the underwear kept us warm when keeping warm was the point. We knew we were among the lucky ones that year, to be stationed in Nancy behind the lines.

At the time, the front stretched about ten miles northeast, toward the Vosges foothills. Not far from those protective ridges, the feverish American race across France after D-Day had come to a halt when the armored divisions of Patton's Third Army ran out of supplies. By mid-October, the weary tanks and half-tracks sat dormant, waiting for fuel, and the front itself barely moved. The newly arrived American infantry, which had come up to replace the armored divisions, was dug deep into foxholes that pockmarked the French soil like a skin disease, while the Germans, who had been on the run for months— a shocking new experience—faced us at last in an exhausted defense line. It was a near-static confrontation, marked by restless forays by both sides. But the Germans were not demoralized—far from it. The closer they got to the Reich and their own homes, the fiercer they fought. Possibly as a result, they sometimes behaved with the demented logic that often lies at the heart of lost causes.

The lines then were only a couple of hundred yards apart, still partly the stuff of World War I; this unnatural closeness had created a kind of perverse intimacy between the two sides. At the time, I remember hearing crude Teutonic obscenities being shouted at Yank outposts in the middle of the night; sometimes they even sounded weirdly amiable. Were they meant as a joke? Or as an attempt at midnight torture for the terrified Yankee riflemen who couldn't leave their exposed positions between the lines until just before dawn?

Around the same time, a German took a couple of potshots at me when I clambered out of my foxhole in order to defecate—for once out in the open. The German deliberately mis-aimed, I thought, and missed twice as a result. A humane act? A show of sympathy? Or again, a subtle form of torture? I didn't have the answer then and I still don't. And there were other experiences like that; everyone had a story of some kind, the stuff of reassuring anecdotes, what you chose to tell your children later on, if you chose to tell them anything.

Mostly, however, there were more conventional episodes, panic-driven routs for both sides, devastating fire-fights, cunning ambushes, at which the Germans excelled, small-scaled massacres. That kind of thing was common in the fall of 1944. Its chief purpose, at least for the Yanks, was to maintain the military status quo, while the Red Ball express rushed fuel and ammunition to the front, where the Third Army was waiting. Nobody was going anywhere without supplies, anyway, certainly not the Americans. The American Army rarely made a move unless its supply lines were in near-perfect order. In any conventional strategic sense, all was relatively quiet in Alsace-Lorraine, as the bulletins used to state with such fatuous serenity. All was quiet northeast of Nancy.

I HAD come to the 26th Division a year before through the Army Specialized Training Program, the ASTP, along with a thousand other teen-age troops. All of us were smart kids. Our arrival was intended to bring the division up to full strength before it shipped overseas. It didn't seem to matter that we were untested for combat, even though we had trained for the infantry during the previous summer, just after our induction into the Army, on the scorching sands of Fort Benning, Georgia. That bothered few in the 26th. Live bodies that moved were what the division seemed to want; their credentials were less important. One of the ASTPs I knew, a painter who later became nationally known, was reported to be blind in one eye; no one, to my knowledge, ever questioned the fact or worried about it, except possibly the artist himself. When it came time for him to fire his rifle, he aimed it just like everyone else.

Nevertheless, the 26th had a reputation to uphold, in the way of most infantry divisions. It was actually the New England National Guard, famous as the Yankee Division in its home territory, with a celebrated World War I record that included action at both St.-Mihiel and Belleau Wood; for its bravery on the Western Front, the 104th regiment of the division won the Croix de Guerre, the first ever awarded an American unit by the French. This record was patriotically nourished by the division between the two World Wars. There were ongoing reunions, banquets, meetings, and publications to reinforce morale. All this was more than a matter of upholding simple pride. Something essential, involving caste and status, was also part of it. For some veterans, contact with the YD represented one way of finally being able to feel like a real American, of feeling comfortable at last within a rigid society that had long been run—sometimes ruthlessly—by Puritans and Brahmins. That was New England then.

But by 1944 there were no longer many true Yankees in the Yankee Division. The New England Irish held on, strong as ever, but with the onset of the draft other ethnic and national groups had begun to infiltrate the roster: provincial Italians, for example, who in those days spoke to no one but other Italians; Armenians, Greeks, Hispanics, Maltese, other ghettoized Mediterraneans. Tagging along was a substantial cluster of despised WASPs, who didn't yet know that they were a symptom of the future, as well as a handful of isolated Jews, who were also despised; but, unlike the WASPs, the Jews were quite used to it. The point was that they were all Yankees now, by regional fiat—Irish, Mediterranean, WASPs, and Jews—and they were slowly becoming passionate cultural egalitarians as well, especially when it came to their own.

AFTER surviving infantry basic at Fort Benning, my ASTP class was sent north to the University of Maine in the winter of 1943 so that we could continue our academic careers. (They, too, had all been drafted straight out of college.) The Army's idea was to turn us into professional engineers in time for the invasion of Japan. Whatever the Army had in mind for us, it turned out to be an easy and comfortable war up there in the heavy snows of Orono, Maine, totally without hassle or anxiety or even hierarchical distinctions. I don't remember any officers on campus, for example, although there had to be a few around. We all went to class happily, we studied, and we never looked back. I was even maintaining an A average in every course, including advanced calculus, a subject that I had already failed at Johns Hopkins. I was even less interested in engineering than I was in medicine, but, of course, in the ASTP it was engineering or nothing. In any case, the war was elsewhere, far from Orono, Maine, and that was how we preferred it.

The Army Specialized Training Program couldn't last. We knew that. After only two months, Congress voted it out of existence, under sharp pressure from rebellious constituents, who claimed that we were being coddled; it was the old populist cry of elitism. As it happened, folding the program turned out to be most convenient for the Army, surprising none of us. The boys of ASTP would provide a trained pool of 18- and 19-year-old infantrymen—

175,000 in all, from schools all over the country—to fill out lean divisions like the Yankee Division in time for the invasion of Europe and for what might follow.

We turned in our books, packed up our duffel bags, and said good-bye, feeling sad and betrayed (easy enough when you're eighteen). We were also scared, which was soon to be our common, ongoing state, even more so because we were still without clear orders. But soon enough, within only a couple of days, we were on our way by train to Tennessee, where we were told that the Yankee Division was bivouacked in the middle of spring maneuvers. I had to check a map to find out exactly where Tennessee was.

As soon as we arrived, we were sucked into the innards of the division, whose officers and non-commissioned officers could hardly believe their eyes when they saw us. New meat, in their hungry words, fresh beef, and young (virginal, too, in most cases), a windfall of malleable human flesh when it was really needed. No division could ask for more.

As for me, I was assigned to the first squad, third platoon of C Company, 104th regiment, former winner of the Croix de Guerre. At that point, C Company, like many other companies in the Yankee Division, was severely understrength, although not catastrophically so, as it would be just six months later, in October of 1944.

CAPTAIN Michael Antonovich commanded C Company, but only in a manner of speaking, as I liked to think. And I was not the only one with doubts about him. Everyone in the company had them, including the non-commissioned officers. Antonovich had pursued his mandate in standard fashion, joining ROTC while in college, then entering Officer Candidate School after he was drafted, and finally, as he moved up the ladder, finding his present post in the Yankee Division, which needed young officers as much as it needed enlisted men.

Almost everything that Antonovich knew about military operations he had picked up from someone else, mostly in school, sometimes in the field. It was all secondhand, by the numbers, memorized. But secondhand knowledge was a commonplace among Army officers then; the Army was building an officer corps in quick-time and moved accordingly. Naturally, there were anomalies. The fact was that Michael Antonovich had never fired a real weapon beyond target practice. His head was stuffed with standard infantry tactics, out of textbooks; some of those tactics went back to the Civil War. He was strapped and bound by the Army's wartime limitations but not unhappily. It suited Antonovich to try to be what he had observed in others and not to venture too far on his own.

Antonovich was from Columbus, Ohio—not from New England—a former football tackle at one of those vast Midwestern state universities: Nebraska or Kansas, I never got it straight. He looked the part, too, with a massive body, thick legs, and a square-skulled head that carried a dense, unhappy expression around the eyes whenever he was expected to think clearly. At those moments, his right eye tended to wander slightly, perhaps from the strain. Whatever, this walleyed effect could be disconcerting when C Company came face-to-face with it.

The cruel fact that everybody understood about Michael Antonovich was that he was mentally out-ofsynch with his physical capabilities. He could run faster than most of us. He could lift weights that were beyond our reach and outlast almost anyone in C Company on forced marches. This is not inconsiderable for the head of an infantry company, who must always at least appear to excel. But Antonovich wasn't really intelligent enough to be a company commander—not that brilliance is needed for the job, although soundness is. As it was, the captain lacked both. His judgments were too often unreliable, as though he was depending on guesswork, and he indulged, again too often, in the unpleasant discriminatory habit of playing favorites. (I was never one of them nor were any of my pals.) This left some of us nervous in Captain Antonovich's presence. We never knew what to expect of him, and my guess is that he didn't either. Not auspicious, I thought, from the first meeting.

Under Antonovich, Francis J. Gallagher served as third platoon lieutenant. Gallagher came from a small milltown near Worcester, Massachusetts, a National Guard enlistee who had been tapped for OCS early on and eventually graduated near the top of his class. Gallagher was only five feet four, very small for an officer, very small for a man, with shanks like fishbones and a frame as delicate as a cobweb—a marked physical type, exactly the reverse of Michael Antonovich. And the two officers were opposites in many other ways, too, which was, perhaps, a touch of good fortune for us. Unlike the captain, for example, who sometimes seemed to be sleepwalking as he led his company on parade, Gallagher was all feist and snap, with a little man's high-pitched tenor that keened jokes and good-natured barbs at anyone who got in his way. That included Captain Antonovich and higher ranks as well, without too much discrimination or intimidation on Gallagher's part.

Gallagher was not shy. We liked it that he never hesitated, never dallied. You only had to come on him unexpectedly out in the field where he would be squatting over a slit trench, pants down around his ankles, his buttocks the size of tennis balls, it seemed, while the turds dropped out of him without apparent preparation or struggle. No, there was no shyness there. In that primitive position, unfazed and unself-conscious, he was like a perfect miniature B-26 calmly releasing its bombs through an open bay onto the earth below, and we marked him as an ace for it.

Wisely enough, Gallagher and Antonovich kept their distance from each other. We rarely saw them together. It was as though they had decided that ordinary social contact would produce an irreparable, head-on collision. (Sooner or later, differences in temperament and sensibility would effectively do the job.) When all else failed, as it often did in the Army, Antonovich tended to fall back on hysteria, like so many oversized men. While Antonovich screamed and his right eye wandered, Gallagher, in the same situation, merely grew shrill. I found the contrast between the two officers interesting. It quickly began to assume aspects of an athletic contest, and I soon was taking sides in any conflict that involved the two of them, rooting my favorite on as the game proceeded, for it was still a game at that point, before we landed in France. At the time I write of, Captain Antonovich and Lieutenant Gallagher could still occasionally joke with each other in front of us, however they might really feel. On the other hand, I don't know what passed between them when C Company was not around to observe the action. Presumably plenty.

Between Antonovich and Gallagher stood the bandy-legged figure of Rene Archambault, the company's master sergeant. Archambault, who was from Presque Isle, Maine, and claimed partial Indian ancestry, was one of those men who are always dissatisfied with the world: a chronic complainer. He was also one of those who insist on trying to fix it: a chronic meddler. Maybe that's the nature of master sergeants, for whom everything exists to be corrected. For example, he was not happy with the name Rene. It was too sissy for him; and sissy marked the depths of contempt in Rene Archambault's Army, as everywhere else. How well the smart ASTP kids knew it, and how often our master sergeant liked to remind us of it. I think he probably also disliked his family name, which he pronounced as they would in France: "Arr-chahm-bow." Spoken with the merest suggestion of self-mockery, as though he expected us to laugh at it. He wanted everyone to call him Arch, insisting on it, in fact, in what we all perceived as an attempt at false intimacy. We were uncomfortable with that, always.

Arch was a steady, compulsive worker—also part of the nature of master sergeants—issuing orders in a surprisingly reedy voice that was not unlike Lieutenant Gallagher's, scurrying around on his bandy legs, glaring at us over his scimitar nose, which in profile made a perfect half-moon arc. Such perfection in noses is not given to most men. Perhaps it was part of his Penobscot heritage.

I think of poor self-conscious Arch, going through life having to pronounce his name slowly, syllable by syllable, then spell it out for everyone he was meeting for the first

time: the tedium of it, the resentment. I could sympathize
with that. I had been spelling my name for strangers for
years. I even had to do it for Rene Archambault, twice.

We all belonged to the three of them, Antonovich, Gallagher, and Archambault, and on their own terms. Company C and the third platoon was their common property.
For better or worse. To make or break. Life and death, in
fact. And few questions, of any kind, were ever allowed us,
even by Francis Gallagher. As Rene Archambault used to
say, standing over us with his hands on his hips, as though
his words would explain everything, "There's a war to be
won out there, you dumb fucks." Spoken with a cheerless
smile, too.

Such were our leaders.


AND the first squad and its leader?

I find that I have to struggle to get the names right after
all these years. I have to reach deep down for them, dig-
ging into the marshy pit of memory. When the names surface, if they surface at all, they must then be tested against
the accumulation of a half-century of other names, and I
don't feel especially confident about the process.

Doug Kelleher, then (ASTP), Bern Keaton (also ASTP),
and the others, Roger Johnson, Paul Willis, Barney Barnato, and Rocky Hubbell (actually and unforgettably, J.
Rutherford Hubbell, Jr.), who was our squad leader.

No one in the first squad ever called Rocky Hubbell
"Rutherford." There were too many comic overtones to the
name, too many possible easy shots. He himself tended to
joke about it. "I'm saving Rutherford for my old age," Rocky
used to say. "Like capital," he would add, raising a laugh.

But all those names covered a nice range, Kelleher, Keaton, Kotlowitz, Willis, Barnato, and the others, somehow wholly appropriate for an army of draftees. If I have them right, that is. If I didn't invent some of them in the passion to remember. Also, I've discovered that I get a little heated when I write the names out like this. A small tremor of nervous agitation seems to go through me, and I shiver a little.

AS SOON as we arrived in the hills of Tennessee from the University of Maine, Rene Archambault co-opted us. That was his right as master sergeant of C Company but not necessarily his duty. (Master sergeants can do anything they want.) What Arch did was to make Doug Kelleher, Bern Keaton, and me the squad's BAR team, the three-man Browning Automatic Rifle unit. This happened almost as soon as we detrained, just minutes after we had been assigned to the third platoon; and it did not thrill us.

To begin with, the life expectancy of the BAR team in combat, we had learned at Fort Benning, was about eleven seconds. (That is not hyperbole, it is scientific fact.) Then the BAR itself was an unusually clumsy weapon, which everyone rightly tried to avoid, halfway between a machine gun and a rifle, a deadweight all the way. Among the three of us, we would be carrying one BAR, two M-1 rifles, ammo for all three, and a cluster of hand grenades. That was Arch's welcoming gift to us. Doug was made team leader, Bern and I were the assistants; on marches we would share the weapon, rotating it among us every couple of miles.

No, we were not thrilled.

Then, as soon as Arch finished with us, he swept through the rest of the company, repeating the first squad's shuffle, getting the old National Guardsmen and aging draftees off the hook, freeing them of the terrible burden of the Browning Automatic Rifle. (He had made Roger Johnson and Paul Willis, who were a two-man BAR team before we got there, happy GIs with a single order.) It was a pretty slick operation. Eventually most of the BARs in the Yankee Division ended up in the hands of the smart new arrivals from ASTP.

It was easy to read the future in that. We would be the division's stooges, heirs to every unwanted job, the BAR to begin with, and KP, guard, and latrine duty as well. It would be a kind of stupid hazing with no recourse, and we would be its victims. Of course, we had to accept it, cursing among ourselves like big shots, and sounding like children.

But part of me, at eighteen, was eager to suffer the hazards and humiliations of war. In fact, I thought I had it coming to me. I was burning with a young man's need to please and with a secret touch of patriotic fervor, two strong motives for performing without complaint. Also, as I've said, I really hated the Germans. It was a deeply personal loathing, not abstract at all, with powerful political impulses that had been inflamed by reports of concentration camps, *Kristallnacht,* and venomous anti-Semitism. And I was a Jew. In terms of motive, that went a long way in those days.

FOR THE moment, after arriving in Tennessee, we were all despondent. We had been wrenched out of a safe environment at the University of Maine. Our names had been neatly arranged in alphabetical order and divvied up among various battalions, thrusting Kelleher, Keaton, and Kotlowitz together for the first time, although we had known each other on the Orono campus by sight. My real pals from basic training and Maine, my old buddies, were also being clustered in alphabetical niches, "A"s with "A"s, "B"s with "B"s, and so on to the very last Zed.

I soon learned that Kelleher was an Army brat, son of a career officer, a colonel sitting out the war behind a desk at Fort Dix, New Jersey, while Keaton was a parochial-school kid from Hackensack, New Jersey, who was suffering his first religious doubts, mostly in silence. I wasn't much interested in Kelleher and Keaton, and they weren't much interested in me—not at first. I wanted my old Orono buddies back, those who understood me and loved me without question, and they were gone now to other squads in other platoons, scattered by the necessities of the alphabet.

But given time and experience enough, of course, Doug Kelleher and Bern Keaton quickly became my buddies, too, understanding me possibly too well, and the eczema that had flared up on the back of my neck and the insides of my elbows, whenever I remembered where I was, soon cleared up, leaving only a scab or two as reminders of my arrival in Tennessee in the Yankee Division. Nevertheless, there was no doubt about it: I was in the infantry, for real. That knowledge—so bitter, so conclusive—would be like living with a stone in my gut.


AND the rest of the squad?

Roger Johnson and Paul Willis, relieved of the BAR by Arch's masterstroke, became our scouts. They both seemed comfortable in the job; as scouts, they were always up front, a touch away from everybody else—a job that was good for the human-shy, which they both were. Johnson, in fact, was so taciturn that he was often speechless, literally without words, a Green Mountain boy from Vermont who spoke perhaps half a dozen sentences a day, mainly having to do with his personal needs. And Paul Baxter Willis?

Paul Willis was the company thief, one with a specific and highly original taste. He stole only our laundry, concentrating on underwear. That is all Willis ever took. Underwear. A weird and feckless act, stealing another man's underwear—and not easy to understand.

I have tried for years to imagine how such a kink shapes itself, but without success. I know that there must be psychoanalytic explanations—more than one, probably—but such explanations are not always as humanly satisfying as I might want. So I try to avoid them. And if there was an erotic subtext to Willis's thievery, I was too naive then to grasp it. Now I wonder what Willis himself thought of it all, something that didn't occur to me at the time. Did he try to set his thieving apart from his real self, as a temporary aberration that was out of his control? Or did he rationalize his right, in *Übermensch* style, to steal from his comrades?

We tried to confront Willis once—Kelleher, Keaton, and I—stumbling foolishly through our accusations, losing confidence as we went along. But Willis was ahead of us. He denied the charge without hesitation, without a blink, smiling rigidly the whole time, as though his mouth was trapped in a vise. Dismay and disbelief filled his watery-blue eyes. His body shied from us. Me? Willis mimed, refusing to speak aloud as he held the flat of his hand over his heart as though his heart had been wounded. Slowly then, the concept of pathology, its repulsive reality, which I knew only from the classroom, began to form in my mind. The same thing, I think, was happening to Kelleher and Keaton. There stood skinny Paul Willis in the middle of the barracks floor, dressed only in Bern Keaton's olive drab shorts, which just happened to be his size. They even had Bern's laundry mark on them. And still smiling, still theatrically mute, as pale, willowy, and dim as Hamlet's Ophelia, Willis continued to deny that they were Bern's.

This offended us. We became morally indignant. And smug. (Didn't Willis's "crime" prove our superiority to the old-timers in the YD?) We began to avoid him, as though he carried something contagious on his person. Rocky Hubbell, to whom we finally complained as our squad leader, advised us to look the other way. It was only underwear, he said blandly. In time, I came to understand that this was excellent counsel, although I disdained it at first. Willis, I began to reason to myself, was one of our scouts. At some moment in a dubious future, some critical moment, we might all have to depend on his judgment and his good will, perhaps for our very lives. That idea made me rethink everything. I decided that I would allow Paul Willis to be a thief. I would have to.

Besides, Rocky Hubbell did not like confrontations. Not in his squad. Given an option, he always avoided a verbal shoot-out. Steadiness was what Rocky admired. Rocky, who was a tall, bony Texan, the first I had ever known, still had something of the romantic look of the old west about him, something dusty and a little raw. He barely moved his lips when he spoke, so you had to listen hard to hear what he was saying; this, of course, kept everybody at full attention. One of his pleasures was to write sentimental love letters to his girlfriend in Amarillo. Sprawled on his barracks cot in the evening for hours at a time, he composed these notes with meticulous care, chewing on his pencil and staring into space, perhaps looking for the muse. Sometimes he tested a phrase on us, asking for approval from Bern Keaton or me, whom he considered the squad's arbiters of culture, thereby confirming our own opinions of ourselves. "The beautitudes [sic] of God's blessings" is one I recall, with gratitude. This unexpected poetic thrust in Rocky made us feel close to him; any sign of softness in our NCOs or officers had the same effect.

Inevitably, I guess, there had to be an opposing force at work in Rocky, if only for symmetry's sake. With Rocky it took the form of a chaotic impulse hidden just below the surface. We all felt its power at one time or another, and it could be scary. Rocky's explosions, when they erupted, generated such heat and electricity that he would later have to pretend that he couldn't remember what had happened; they were too much to acknowledge for a man who contrived to live in such an aura of sanity most of the time. A report of a crazed gunfight in a Columbia, South Carolina, alley once: nobody hurt. An extended joyride in a stolen car outside the same city just before we went overseas: no charges pressed. And others, later on. They were all forgiven, it seems, in light of Rocky's military record, which was without flaw. Lieutenant Gallagher intended to keep it that way; squad leaders as competent as Rocky Hubbell were rare. Nevertheless, once we had developed reservations about his behavior, we learned to keep an eye

on him. We needed him, as we needed Paul Willis, at his
sanest and most effective, when he was feeling fully
responsible for us and himself, when there were no dis-
tractions.

Another interesting thing about Rocky: he didn't like to
show himself naked in front of the squad. This forced him
into a whole set of embarrassed contortions whenever he
dressed or undressed in the barracks with us, something
that was comical at times in his efforts to keep from being
seen, as though he were a virginal maiden like Susanna,
nervous at being spied on by the elders. (We may not have
been elders, but we were certainly voyeurs.) It also meant
that he was usually the last man in the showers, joining us
only when we were almost done, standing with his back to
the rest of us, soaping himself slowly, as he pretended to
be lost in thought. That too made him unexpectedly vulnerable.

"Small penis," Doug Kelleher decided.

"No penis," Bern Keaton said.

And we all laughed, perhaps too loudly, in the tradi-
tional way of slaves who think they're smarter than their
master.

As for Barney Barnato, he never did make it back to the
division in time for Tennessee maneuvers. He was still on
emergency leave in Bridgeport, Connecticut, where his
mother had been dying for three weeks. That was the story
at the time. Poor Barney Barnato, we thought, remembering our own mothers; it was sad. That left just six of us in
the first squad for maneuvers, something more than half
strength, if my count is right and if I can forget Ira Fedderman and the others who only joined us after maneuvers
were over.

# TWO

# Crossing the Cumberland

WE WERE encamped east of Nashville. Once we had been swallowed up by the first squad and handed the hated BAR, three days of a steady, chilled rain made life even more miserable for us and kept the Yankee Division from moving out into the sodden Tennessee hills that surrounded the camp. In those hills, we were to search out and destroy an unknown "enemy" division that had already arrived on the scene somewhere and was waiting for us in hiding. That at least was the rumor that spread through C Company. The scenario, which made room for a certain amount of improvisation, was simple enough. The encounter between us, the fake battle that had been planned for so long between the two divisions, was to be to the finish, theirs or ours. It was serious business, in Army terms, and one of the final steps in our training before heading overseas.

The decision was made at Division Headquarters to bivouac where we were until the rains lifted. Meanwhile we soaked in our wet uniforms, the coarse wool of socks and sweaters sticking to our skins and stinking. It was late April in Tennessee and felt like mid-winter, and the fact that it was already spring by the calendar turned our mood even more sour. We hung around the cooking fires making grim jokes, sipping coffee so hot that we could hardly hold the scalding canteens in our bare hands, watching our clothes steam in the heat of the flames. Shivering like animals, we felt sorry for ourselves and swore at the world for being imperfect, forgetting why we were in Tennessee in the first place; ideology was suddenly no match for bodily comforts.

During that time, Bern Keaton and I shared a pup tent, a logical pairing on the surface, you would think, ordered by Rocky in good faith, but it turned out to be a match made in hell. The problem was that I was not entirely competent at meeting certain basic military demands, a curse that followed me everywhere I served in the Army. For example, I never learned how to dig an efficient drainage ditch around our tent—an ordinary job for almost anyone else—so that rainwater, instead of innocently running off from our quarters as it should have, poured through the tent itself, soaking blankets, clothes, rifles, ammo, and us. When this happened, Bern and I stared at the fierce little streams that swept through our shelter, then turned to each other, stricken. Was he blaming me? Should he blame me? Could I defend myself? These terrible questions hovered silently in the air while guilt riddled my eyes and Bern looked away in disgust.

By the second night, the tent itself was leaking through its overhead seams (not my fault, not anybody's), and soon, as the dismal wet hours slowly passed, Bern Keaton and I awoke to the discovery that we could not bear the other's presence. By mid-morning we had begun to hate each other. It was the kind of smoldering loathing that flares up when misery is not only shared but created by two people bound to each other by necessity (the sad story of many marriages). Bern's flatulence turned out to be another problem, although, to be absolutely fair, he was later to make the same charge against me, with some accuracy.

We also watched anxiously as the others, the National Guardsmen and the old draftees—Paul Willis and Rocky Hubbell, as well as Roger Johnson, who turned out to be superbly skilled in the art of living in the wild—stayed reasonably dry, ate well, and actually seemed to be enjoying themselves at moments. Of course, it was a class thing. I—and Bern, too—was soft from birth and from training. Neither of us had been exactly used to receiving hard knocks in our other lives, although we were fast developing a stoic mode to help us face them in the Army. And while we were learning, our wounds were being rubbed sore by the fact that Doug Kelleher, who was also soft, was sharing Roger Johnson's tent, a model of basic engineering achievement that stood high and dry only a couple of yards from ours.

Another day passed like this, filled with lighter rain and considerably thicker fog, through which we wandered ectoplasmically and tried to stay warm. On the fourth day, we awoke to a sun finally streaming down from the east, over the hills we were eventually supposed to occupy. A sudden golden warmth descended from a cloudless sky—spring at last. We greeted it by taking off our shirts and basking in the morning air for a few minutes, Doug Kelleher scratching his ribs and making gorilla noises, which were his specialty. It was a couple of moments of unexpected joy, but almost immediately the order came through to strike tents and pack up—on the double, Rocky added. Within an hour, after a sloppy breakfast eaten on the run, we began to move out, full-field packs bouncing on our shoulders. Even for us, who were specialists in speed, this was quick-time.

Arch's thin voice piped out full-strength from up front of the company column. Hup-tup, hup-tup, his usual barking sound. Michael Antonovich and Francis Gallagher and a couple of other officers stood at the side of the road, watching us dogstep off. As we marched along, Antonovich thrust out his chin and jabbed his right fist into the palm of his left hand, which was always a sign of excitement in him. I think he was trying to give us the eager eye for the battle that lay ahead, as he had been taught to do by his OCS instructors, hoping, by his look and stance, to generate a kind of fierce energy in his troops at the idea of meeting the enemy. (A lost cause in the first squad, as he should have known.) Gallagher, on the other hand, was nattering out of the side of his mouth to one of his fellow officers from the second platoon, paying little attention to his troops.

Hup! cried Arch, placing himself between Antonovich and Gallagher. As we passed them, Rocky, leading our stunted column, offered a good-humored mock salute that Gallagher instantly returned in kind. They were clearly in high spirits. Meanwhile our scouts marched ahead and we brought up the tail of the squad. Doug Kelleher was carrying the BAR for the first couple of miles and the rifle, slung from his shoulder, barrel down, seemed almost as tall as he was. Bern and I shared the ammo with him, heavy clips of fat rounds looped around our skinny waists like metal corsets, bandoleers draped dramatically across our thin shoulders and over our chests, with a few grenades hanging from our belts. Armed to the teeth, thanks to the machinations of Master Sergeant Rene Archambault. We looked ludicrous.

Before we were a mile out, I heard the leader of the second squad, a couple of yards behind us, call out, "Close it up, Fedderman. Close it up, goddammit." I knew that refrain. I had been hearing it ever since we had trained together at Fort Benning. Fat, clever Ira Fedderman, who never moved fast enough, wherever he was—Benning, Maine, or Tennessee—and was always shat on for it. But I had to watch my sympathies. Fedderman, an expert at many unexpected things, knew how to play on them. Earlier, just after we arrived in Tennessee, he had chosen Bern and me as his spiritual escape from the goons of the second squad, of which he was a more than shaky member. I had to be careful.

Nevertheless, our foul mood had begun to lift. Cheerfulness spread through the ranks as we moved along. Bern and I no longer hated each other. I forgave him; I'm sure he forgave me. I even heard Bern, who kept treading on my heels, begin to sing under his breath. *"This will be . . . my shi-ning . . . hour . . ."*

"For Chrissakes, Bern."

"What's wrong?"

"You're stepping all over me."

"So pick it up."

It was 9:30 in the morning, the sun was on the rise, and we were on our way to the fake wars. Good riddance to the heavy litter we had left behind in our muddy camp. We had turned it into a dump.

WE COVERED about nine miles during daylight—not a little, certainly not a lot. At some point after dark on that first day, we should have stopped to bivouac for the night. There seemed to be no real hurry, and no real destination to reach. Also, the company line had become stretched out. This was not unusual. It almost always resulted from the varying rates of speed at which each platoon and each squad and sometimes each man marched. Therefore the chronic cry "Close it up, Fedderman!" could always be heard—or Keaton, Kelleher, or Kotlowitz, for Fedderman was certainly not the only one at fault here. We were all erratic stumblers at times.

Toward midnight, then, still marching at an increasingly slack pace, we were attacked on our right flank by invisible units of the enemy division, which were hiding in the dark. We should not have been surprised, but we were. Fake ammo suddenly began to pop in front of us like cap pistols; toy explosives detonated to the right, throwing up clods of wet soil; a dozen red flares, looking gorgeous as they fanned out in the night sky, lighted the Tennessee hills to the north. I could see the shocked look on Doug Kelleher's face when all the racket began. A rush of strange noises rolled down the hills on our right, a rattling of weapons and ammo, the heavy sound of men running and trying to shout at the same time. I even thought I heard a dog barking wildly in the middle of it all.

I froze. Everybody in the first squad froze. Johnson, Willis, and Rocky Hubbell were positioned somewhere up front, yards ahead of us, gathered in a tight cluster. At that moment, a lump of hard dirt hit me on the shoulder and pebbles rolled off my pack. "Holy shit!" Bern Keaton called out, and fell to the ground behind me. Up ahead, Doug Kelleher did the same. When the BAR hit the ground, it sounded as though it had broken in two.

"Return fire, first squad. Close in!" That was Rocky, shouting stilted orders. Close in where? Fire at whom?

The detonations came closer, grew louder. I could smell the unmistakable odor of real danger. A stone hit my helmet. Way up front, Michael Antonovich was screaming something. Above his voice I could hear Gallagher's Irish tenor rattling away. Then Arch's own blustery voice cut through it. What were they shouting? In what language? Standing there in the dark, immobilized and disoriented, we were discovering the true chaos that defines almost every military action.

Perhaps a minute passed, filled with the noise of weapons firing fake ammo at us. There were another couple of flares to the north. Then there was a silence, a great black vacuum, empty of sound, so sudden that it felt as though it had been agreed upon in advance. (Perhaps it had.)

"Hit the ground," an unknown voice called out from our right. "All of you." The voice sounded very calm, very authoritative—amplified, too, as though its owner were speaking through a bullhorn. "Put your weapons aside," it

continued, enunciating each word carefully. "You are pris-
oners of war, captives of the 78th infantry division. Pay
strict attention to what I say. I will not say it twice. I don't
want anybody to get hurt."

I believed in that voice and trusted it. Even more, I
secretly wanted it to take complete charge of me, to make
me a prisoner of war, a captive of the 78th infantry division. (A loathsome notion, to want to be a POW, as I came
to believe only later.) I placed my M-1 on the ground,
unpeeled all the BAR ammo and laid it neatly alongside
my rifle, glad to be rid of it. Then I did the same with the
M-1 ammo and the grenades. (In the middle distance,
meanwhile, perhaps twenty yards away, I could make out
the dim silhouettes of the enemy, rifles pointing at us; they
were barely visible but fully sensed, rustling presences in
the night.) I did all this deliberately, slipping off my pack,
too, relieved of that at last, moving to a slow beat to quell
my inner excitement, for I was terrifically excited at the
unexpected action. Everyone was, I'm sure. And then suddenly, without thought or preparation, I took off to the left
into the brush, my normally cautious heart charged by a
new energy, my body moving powerfully on its own, as
though it had a life that was separate from the rest of me.

"What the hell," I heard Bern say behind me, his voice
heightened by surprise, but it was too late. I was gone.


I SLEPT the night away about a mile or so to the west,
well up in the hills that rose sharply on that side of the valley. During the climb, a sapling's branch had snapped back
against my left eye, causing swelling, which I kept poking
at until it hurt.

I soon settled down and decided to try to make myself comfortable. There weren't a lot of options. I had been trained to use my helmet liner as a pillow. I turned a pile of leaves and twigs into a primitive mattress. And that was all I had. Then I lay down to try to sleep. The major problem was the chill, which was constant and biting, but there was little I could do about it. I was cold all night, waking fitfully to hug myself and get the blood going; stamping my feet also helped. Exhaustion took care of the rest, quickly putting me back to sleep, although I don't think I was ever fully under, in the conventional sense. In my sleep, I thought I could still hear the sounds of a battle down below. There were intermittent noises all night. I found myself worrying about what had happened to the Yankee Division.

When a leg cramp finally woke me in the morning, I could see the sun hovering behind a mass of gray-black clouds that were barely moving across the bleak sky. Our brief romance with warmth and light was over. It was sure to rain again within the hour. Nevertheless, I was pleased with myself. I was alone amid a vast, wooded space that opened out onto grand vistas on the other side of the valley. There were no orders here to be obeyed, no squad to bother with. And no threats from an unknown "enemy." Still, I began to prepare to return to the third platoon. I stood up, tested my leg, stretched, and rinsed out my mouth with water from my canteen, which was the only piece of equipment left to me. The wind had started up by then, and I hugged myself again for warmth. My sore eye felt tender. I had been out long enough. I had had my little adventure and it felt good.

"Cold, baby?"

I knew that voice. "Keaton," I said, turning around. "You bum."

He laughed. He was sitting on the ground behind me, about twenty feet away. "You don't look too happy to see me," he said.

"How'd you find me, anyway?"

"I tailed you. Like the deerslayer. I could hear you from fifty yards away. Some Indian you'd make." He laughed again. Then he stood up and, turning his back, began to pee. Walking over to him, I did the same. Together, back-to-back, we made serious morning noises.

Then the two of us stared into the distance, into the grand hillside vistas, where carpets of Tennessee clover seemed to go on forever. Down below, behind a stand of trees, a few columns of smoke rose in the air on the road we had marched on until midnight.

We watched the smoke rise. Bern seemed sad. So did I. I felt a tug, a sudden gloomy sense that maybe we were in the wrong place.

"You think we should go in?" Bern asked.

I made a face.

"Yes or no?" he said.

"I'm hungry," I said. "And I'm cold. I have a swollen eye. Do I need all this?"

We moved off just as it began to rain again. I was limping a little from my cramp. The whole sky was now gray-black. Even the delicious Tennessee clover, rippling in sweet waves in the heavy wind, was beginning to look gray. There was not a house or a shed, no habitation of any kind in sight. We were totally alone. The rain persisted, however, very fine in the early morning, misty and still soft, not yet ready to offer the wild drenching that would soon descend on the area of our so-called maneuvers where Bern Keaton and I were wandering so aimlessly and amateurishly. But we kept going, trying to catch a glimpse of the hidden road below, dreaming of food and warmth, while almost straight ahead, although we didn't know it yet, lay the broad, brooding sweep of the Cumberland River, already in full spring flood.

BY MID-MORNING we were drifting down toward the road, hating each other again. There was nothing we could do about it. We were like two Pavlovian animals, enslaved by our oppressed reflexes, and, as I've suggested, between Bern and me misery usually brought resentment. Besides, the sight of fresh smoke rising in the morning air from the road below reminded us of how hungry we really were. We had not eaten in sixteen hours. I had reached the point of blaming Bern; I'm sure he blamed me.

We slipped onto the road amid strangers. Company C? we asked. Wrong company, wrong battalion. We were then pointed in the right direction, toward the rear, by a couple of ASTPs who recognized us, and we started on our way back to the platoon. As far as I could tell, there was no sign of the 78th Division today. It was just a long, disorderly line of YD troops from the 104th regiment, most of them half-dressed and unshaven, chewing away on C or K rations, sipping hot coffee, and smoking cigarettes from little cardboard boxes that came with the rations. As we moved along, my wool sweater hugged me like a wet sheet. Bern suffered the same clinging mess. "Jesus," he kept complaining, pulling at himself. At least the rain had stopped, momentarily.

In another few moments, I recognized a couple of faces from A Company, then B. When we reached C, a little throb of joy, mixed with a touch of fear, rose in my throat. Really home! Would we be welcomed or punished?

From the side of the road, Ira Fedderman called out a greeting. He was sitting in his underwear on a blanket, hugging his chubby knees, with another blanket wrapped around him while his clothes dried on the ground alongside him. On his face, which was as round as a dinner plate, was a smart little half-smile. Typical. (Fedderman was from Greenwich Village, via Bensonhurst, Brooklyn, a route into the great world that he liked to describe as "a heady descent onto the primrose paths of lower Manhattan"; that was how Fedderman talked.) As we passed him, he began to sing to us, in a voice that was deliberately off-pitch.

*"Lights are low since you went away . . ."* And so on, right to the end of the absurdly lugubrious lyric: *"My buddies . . . my buddies . . . my buddies,"* Fedderman's voice rising with each repetition, like a choirboy's falsetto.

Fedderman was full of such tricks. They got him into a lot of trouble. Other guys didn't quite appreciate them. They were insulted by them, or ticked off. Nobody was immune. It was as though Fedderman couldn't help himself. Occasionally, he would even call Bern and me "Allegro and Penseroso," interchangeably. Fedderman thought the literary allusion would flatter us. But we weren't flattered. We thought it was ridiculous and affected, being called Allegro and Penseroso like that, and it was, even though Fedderman was offering it, in part, as a kind of tribute. Anyway, we pretended Fedderman wasn't there, sitting on the side of the road in his underwear, singing off-key. We looked the other way as we passed him by until he was behind us. We were in no mood for sarcastic ironies.


WITHIN five minutes, soggy on beer, Rocky forgave us. "Such things happen," he said vaguely. (He knew better than I about such matters.) But I wanted more from him. I wanted to be acknowledged a winner. Hadn't I lived to fight another day? Rocky ignored that. "Better take care of that eye," he said, peering at it microscopically.

"You guys were derelict," Rocky went on after a moment, as though we didn't know that. "You ran. And you ran before our counterattack. You guys know there's always a counterattack." I could smell the beer on him, but I thought he sounded reasonable enough. "Now pick up your equipment and no bullshit about it. Over there, the pile behind Willis. And don't forget, this little incident is just one nail in your coffin." Then, after a pause, "And you only get four."

And what happens after four, I wondered, but Rocky's words sounded much tougher than his voice, so I kept quiet. As I said, he forgave us; it was his nature.

There was a mixed welcome from the rest of the squad. Doug Kelleher giggled at us as we gorged our rations, his prep-school ninny giggle, which he never quite learned to master. Johnson was inimitably quiet; not for the first time I wondered if we actually existed for him. Willis was smug and dim. Listening to Kelleher and Willis describe the night's events, we soon learned that Michael Antonovich had rallied the company in the dark after our escape—I guess the screams I had heard from him were some sort of hysterical early signal—and then driven the enemy off, into the hills in the east. To me it sounded crazy, the idea of C Company carrying the day after all seemed lost, but apparently it was true. In fact, for the moment Antonovich was something of a hero in the company, an unusual role for him.

A couple of hours passed before we began to pack up again. This time I took the BAR from Doug, feeling a little apologetic, and he carried my M-1. By then, Bern had cheered up a bit, and I was feeling better, too; all it took was some warm food and a couple of smokes. Just before we moved out, Arch stopped by. He seemed happy to see us back—almost gleeful, in fact. He looked us up and down in a long, slow sweep.

"What the hell do you two think you are, anyway?" he asked, cocking his head to one side, "a couple of smart-ass queers?" Then he laughed. I'm sorry to say that we laughed with him, even as we turned red. Arch certainly had a way with words. He would have had more to say, too—I could see he wasn't quite finished with us—if Lieutenant Gallagher hadn't shown up at that moment. Gallagher was another story. All he said as he ambled up to us, nodding amiably, was "Good run, fellas. I don't know whether to mark you missing in action or AWOL. Any ideas?" That sounded friendly to me and entirely rhetorical. Still amiable and without waiting for an answer, Gallagher then proceeded to other matters. That was how I knew that our little adventure was not going to be held against us.

So once again we were on our way—the infantryman's obsessive habit—C Company's platoons snaking their path along the mud-filthy road, moving downhill now with a steady kinetic rush toward the great river. Dusk came early and by evening we were huddled around a small fire, opening rations once more, our fatigues steaming in the heat, as we waited our turn to cross the Cumberland. Around the same time, the rains began again.

WE WAITED a long time and, even after waiting, our turn to cross never came. Other factors interceded, other calculations, and everything changed.

This is what happened, as I learned during the course of the night. At two o'clock in the morning, in a deluge, twenty YD infantrymen—most of them from Company B, at least half ASTP kids, median age nineteen—set themselves adrift, as planned, in a rubber assault craft from the turbulent southern shore of the Cumberland. The goal was to make it across to the other side, at a point that lay, cove-like, farther down the swollen river, as part of an assault tactic that was one of the essential challenges of our maneuvers.

Nearly half a dozen crossings had already been made by troops of the 104th in the dark, using the powerful drift of the river's current as the chief propellant. All were successful. Two full platoons now waited on the north shore for reinforcements before moving out to flank the enemy; when the flanking movement happened, it would be an assault in force. The rest of the regiment, strung out to the rear on the southern shore of the Cumberland, had been standing in the rain for three hours or more, waiting their turn; this included Company C and the third platoon.

Nothing moved in the dark. Some of us were already asleep on our feet, holding on to the upturned muzzles of our rifles for support and twitching awake every few seconds in order to keep from falling over in the mud. It was a tricky routine, sleeping on our feet in the rain, but it could be done. At the same time, while we slouched on the road in some disorder, there was an evil-sounding undertone of grousing and obscenities and a steady rumble of truck traffic coming from somewhere in the rear. Straight ahead of us, we could hear the river, not too far away, a swift, chugging sound, vibrating soft and loud, that came and went with the rain and wind.

We didn't know where our NCOs and officers were in the wet blackness. Only Rocky was a sure presence, standing fully awake at the head of the squad, somehow looking both benevolent and fierce at the same time. As the hours passed, we kept checking him out up front, for the simple reassurance of seeing him there, rawboned and tall and very intent.

By then, the cooking fires were out. There were no stars, of course, no moon, no light of any kind to give us away or help to prepare our surprise assault on the enemy who, as it turned out (when all the facts were finally produced), was actually encamped on our side of the river, two or three miles to the east. None of us, of any rank in the 104th regiment, knew this. Intelligence was not functioning that night. The fact, which no one understood or even imagined, was that we were crossing the Cumberland into a void, in which no enemy waited for us; where we were blindly headed there *was* no enemy.

After the first attempt to set themselves adrift, the twenty infantrymen, bowed deep under full equipment in their jammed rubber craft, kept swirling back to shore, spun by the current. There was almost no way to control the movement. All the previous crossings had faced the same problem, and they had solved it through stubbornly repeated tries and a certain amount of luck, on which we all depended; there had been no training, ever, in river crossings for the Yankee Division. So the attempt went on, out into the waters again a second and a third time, until the vessel finally caught hold in mid-river and, spinning slowly, headed downstream, as hoped for.

A few seconds passed as the assault boat disappeared into the dark. On shore, another twenty men from Company B moved into position, ready to board their own craft. Then, according to the evidence, there was a shout downriver from the assault boat, barely heard above the sound of the charging waters, and another, soon followed by an eerie silence on both the river and the shore. More time passed, during which a radio message from regimental headquarters was exchanged with the far shore, and a waiting began—not long, just enough to form an ominous judgment. Moments later, as this judgment shaped itself, a tumult started at the debarkation point, a slow awakening by regimental and battalion officers to the indisputable possibility of catastrophe. Everything had suddenly gone crazily awry.

"Facts" began to seep in, claims, contradictions, exaggerations, tall tales, horror stories; believed, not believed, accepted, rejected—the old chaos, reinforced by a powerful new reality. Nothing, however, was seen again that night of the men and the adolescent boys who tried to make the crossing. They had vanished almost without warning, in the impenetrable darkness, sunk apparently by the extra weight of the ordinary infantry equipment they were carrying. It was over in seconds: twenty bodies instantly drowned in fast-running water—a swift and terrible death, in full awareness.

.    .    .

BACK UP our line of march, a nervous tremor, moving like an electric current, shocked us all awake. It was the rumor of disaster, racing at the speed of light. Three rafts had gone under, it was claimed. An entire platoon of B Company had been swallowed up by the waters. The battalion commander, Major Quesada, had broken down and wept in front of his staff when the news was confirmed.

So it went for another three hours, while we still waited, until a line of dusty chalk, the faintest suggestion of light, showed itself in the east. "Rest, men" was the order, the first since midnight. But we were already sprawled in the mud and beginning to hallucinate from shock and lack of sleep. We stayed there until full dawn, shivering from the cold, when word finally came through that it was over. I think it was Rocky who passed the word along. There would be no more crossings, he said. We were finished with the Cumberland. I gave a moan of pleasure at the news, then slept.

THE CALAMITY on the river marked the end of maneuvers. There was no more talk of the enemy or of assaults, no further tactical night marches or encampments. The official umpires, who were hanging around to referee our victories and defeats, turned in their scorecards and removed the armbands that identified them as neutral observers; all planning stopped while the division drew in its breath, waited, and secretly mourned the dead.

For there were no public rituals for the drowned victims. They had simply vanished, without a trace or a memorial. (One of them, Moose Monchick, was an old pal from Maine, and I grieved for him.) The episode was never publicly acknowledged, never discussed with us in any official way, never reviewed with the line troops who might have learned something from it. It always remained at the level of rumor, as roiled and muddy as the waters of the Cumberland that night, and as awesome.

On a primitive level, life quickly returned to normal; that is, it became routinized again, full of the mundane and ordinary—reveille, taps, meals on time, even close order drill, all the steady, reliable glue that holds military life together and gives it a predictable shape. Within days, after drying out on the shores of the river and vainly trying to assimilate what had happened, we were on our way by truck to Camp Jackson, South Carolina, which would be our new base. Maneuvers were officially over.

At Jackson, it was clear, we would be polished down to the soles of our boots, refined, re-outfitted, and generally readied for overseas service. (No one doubted that we would go to the ETO; the Pacific, halfway around the world on the other side of the globe, was unthinkable.) And so we were—in the relative calm of late spring 1944, a time when one day in camp was much like any other—totally defined by routine, while we pursued the trivia of infantry training in the terrific Carolina heat.

The calm, of course, made life easier. It soothed anxieties, dampened foreboding. Time ran together in a blur. The sameness of the days created order. There can be a sweet, healing monotony to Army life when there are no crises at hand. In this benign environment, and almost without our knowing it, without our even thinking about it, the first squad finally began to come together as a func-

tioning combat unit, for better or worse, with an identity
of its own. ASTPs and the others became near-equals at
last. My still unexplained (to me) little caper in Tennessee,
which was Bern's too, helped; it gave us a kind of modest
notoriety in the platoon and created a small reserve of
respect among the old-timers.

It was around this time that Keaton, Kelleher, and I
stopped dominating the KP and latrine-duty rosters,
although we were not able to get rid of the BAR, even on
impassioned application to Rocky. Also, Rocky's authority
had somehow subtly expanded. He now seemed unassail-
able—exactly what the squad needed. At this time, too,
Roger Johnson decided to talk to us, as though a curse had
been lifted, still using, however, as few words as possible.
On occasion, he even offered us gratuitous advice that
made life more comfortable. Even Willis became part of it
to a degree, included for the first time—condescendingly—in our conversations. Perhaps we had learned how
to absorb his strangeness and were now able to put it
behind us. Maybe we had just grown used to him through
exposure and shared experience.

Soon after we got to Camp Jackson, Barney Barnato
finally made it back from his mother's deathbed, causing a
commotion in the barracks. Barney, we discovered, was
something of an icon in the platoon, an anomalous
European-styled sophisticate in his late thirties who liked
to brag about his sex life. Not that bragging about sex was
so unusual in the Army. But Barney's bragging was never
obvious and never crass. It was all done through inference
and implication, with a certain coy edge to his words that
I found vaguely unpleasant. Once Barney had his say, it

was hard to describe exactly what he had been talking about. He mentioned nameless mistresses, suggested mysterious adulterous affairs, eyeing us salaciously the whole time. And the platoon, which lacked the confidence to challenge him where he seemed to be an expert, responded with hilarious enthusiasm.

In this way, Barney helped turn himself into a glamorous figure amid the drabness of barracks life, and he definitely had the rich, flirtatious style for it. Perhaps as a way of sanitizing his other obsessions, Barney also liked to drop intellectual names, Schopenhauer (whom he called "Chopenauer"), Nietzsche, Kant, among others, and could quote from them or pretended he could. "Coitus is chiefly an affair of the man," he once announced to a barracks full of troops. "And pregnancy entirely that of the woman. Chopenauer." A roar went up. "Do you know what coitus is, you ignorant fools?" Another roar. They loved Barney. These nibbles at exotic philosophical flesh were never questioned by any of us; we were like vacuums when it came to philosophy, ready to accept anything that was set in front of us.

Like Paul Willis, Barney was a truly strange man. His body had become totally hairless from an unnamed childhood disease. And he had an unplaceable accent—vaguely mittel-Europa—that I could never identify. He worried me (sexual boasting always does), especially when I learned that his mother hadn't died, after all, that there was even some question about whether she had actually been sick in the first place, and that this had not been Barney Barnato's first emergency furlough, by any means. It all seemed a little peculiar to us, perhaps more than a little.

Bern, in fact, wouldn't go near him and soon Barney began to replace Willis as a pariah for us. I'm sorry to say that we seemed to need one.

Then Doug Kelleher, at the very end of our stay at Jackson, received a special transfer (the kind we all dreamed of), thanks to his father, the career officer, which took him north to Camp Lee, where he would serve out the rest of the war sitting behind a desk, only a few hundred miles from his father's benevolent eye. Lucky Doug: simple envy of him almost poisoned us. When he left, as teary-eyed as a crocodile from sentiment and guilt, he still could not control his sappy little prep-school giggle nor could he hide the sense of relief he felt at being transferred out of the infantry. He was still giggling when we said good-bye.

And then, almost as soon as Doug was gone—that evening, in fact—Ira Fedderman made an unexpected pitch to Rocky for a transfer into the first squad, to fill the new opening. It was obvious that he was overreaching himself in his need to be close to Bern and me, but to our horror, Rocky immediately said yes—an inexplicable aberration of judgment. What was he thinking? Naturally, the second squad did not resist the move. How happy they were to be rid of their sad sack, how crazy they thought we were for taking him, and within days, as soon as the paperwork could be processed, we had our replacement for Kelleher. Bern and I could hardly believe it.

And finally, I was still unable to face the one great obstacle in infantry training for me: the thirty-foot climb up a rope ladder—under full-field pack and rifle—to the top of a rickety wooden structure, then the dizzying descent down the other side. I was terrified of that ladder, had always been terrified of it, from basic training on. The idea of it brought on uncontrollable vertigo, a trembling of limbs that could not be contained. To escape it in basic, I had volunteered for KP or even latrine duty, willing to trade ten minutes of anguish for twelve hours of hard labor; and I considered it a bargain. I did the same at Jackson and never got to test myself. I felt a certain shame at my failure; shame at my chicken's heart, embarrassed that I was something less than the others. At least Bern, who was unexpectedly nimble at going up and down rope ladders, kept his mouth shut about it and didn't ride me—a discreet act of support, I've always thought.

AT THE very end of our stay at Jackson, just before we left for overseas, still ignorant of where we were going, we gathered in full regalia on a hot August afternoon to parade for General Paul, the Yankee Division's commanding officer. Willard Paul was known as "Gangplank Paul" to everyone in the ranks for his outspoken eagerness to get his troops overseas; his hortatory speeches on the subject went back years and still stuck in the minds of the earliest YD recruits. By now the joke had turned back on itself. This time we were really going. Gangplank Paul had had his wish. Our duffel bags were already packed.

The air that day swirled with dust and flags and the confused sound of bugles and drums clashing dissonantly. It was the first time that some of us had ever seen the general; certainly he was nowhere in sight during maneuvers. (In my experience, World War II generals did not like to be eyed by the troops; they seemed to be amazingly shy.)

Captain Antonovich, huge as a Clydesdale, marched at

a dignified step at the head of the company, moving ponderously and steadily, but he blurred the salute as we passed the reviewing stand because he suddenly began to hurry. When this happened, he gave a few embarrassed coughs and seemed to shrink a little. Behind him, old Arch hupped along on his bandy legs, helmet gleaming in the powerful sun. Lieutenant Gallagher paraded alongside the platoon in a uniform that was a size too large for him, making him look even smaller than he actually was, but he kept us laughing with his side-of-the-mouth wisecracks. We must have looked impressive—the company, the battalion, the regiment, the mighty division itself—spread out almost a full mile, end-to-end. I certainly felt impressive to myself for a moment or two, marching along in the middle of that scrubbed and obedient mob.

Afterward, when we had come to rest in front of him, glittering like heroes of Sparta, Gangplank Paul attempted to make a rousing going-away speech into a microphone that turned out to have feedback problems. Everything he said returned to echo in his face. Nor was he able to rouse us much to battle fever—it was probably too late for that—but clearly his words and the sound of his own voice coming back at him did something for his self-esteem. Maybe they helped to wipe out the memory of the Cumberland crossing, which was much on our minds that day. Maybe it helped him to believe that we were really as tough as he claimed we were. Who knows? Maybe Arch was tough, maybe Rocky and a few others were, but not us, not Bern Keaton or me and surely not our new squad member, Ira Fedderman, who stood alongside me, at parade rest, breathing hard after our march. I could smell his sweat in the heat.

Yes, we thought about the Cumberland crossing a lot that day. It had become a talisman of disaster in the Yankee Division, a bleak reminder of what could happen to any one of us in the future. The message it delivered was stern, and we read it clearly and well. I stood there alongside Fedderman in the August sun, dreamily reviewing the events in Tennessee and thinking of my pal Moose Monchick, who had drowned in the Cumberland with all the rest. Moose Monchick was the drollest person I had ever known, his face always puckered, as though he couldn't decide whether to laugh or cry. Ultimately, of course, he always laughed. God knows, he made us laugh, at Benning and in Maine, with his mostly self-deprecating wit. Anyway, I was thinking about him, in an abstract way, while Gangplank Paul droned on about his ambitions for us, and I had to catch myself. I was beginning to work myself into an emotional state (easy for me), and I did not like emotional states; they gave me hives.

So the day proceeded. We grew tired. There was muttering in the ranks, a plaintive threat of rebellion that passed quickly. At the end of the ceremony, sweltering and dusty with sand, we all nevertheless felt an irresistible sense of pride in ourselves, as the Army had always intended. Even Fedderman, smiling in disbelief at my side, felt it, and at least for this moment he was exactly like everyone else, an infantryman for better or worse. Once we broke ranks, I never saw Gangplank Paul again. It was as though he disappeared from the face of our parade grounds into a no-man's-land of his own, where he could manage the troops from a hidden headquarters, curtained off from the rest of us, like the Wizard of Oz.

That, in any case, was how it came to appear to some of us in the Yankee Division.


AT THE last moment, a few strangers showed up to fill out the platoon. Second and third squads suddenly went to full strength, a startling novelty. Two vague and somewhat reserved individuals, Ralph Natale and George Brewster, joined the first squad, giving us a roster of nine. At last, we all thought, eyeing the newcomers with a cold eye. They were neither ASTPs nor old-timers. Just two poor saps, called replacements, who had been squeezed through the tight pipeline of Army commands, from one outfit to another, ever since they had finished basic training. At last they had found a home. I don't think I ever spoke more than ten words to either of them, or they to me, but at least the squad had put on a little needed fat; with their arrival, we weren't scarecrow-thin anymore.

# THREE

| |
|---|
| *Bliss It Was* |

STILL, it was a kind of bliss to be nineteen then, in uniform, and packed atom-like with all my pals from the Yankee Division aboard the SS *Argentina,* a former luxury cruise liner that had been transformed into a model troopship, as we sailed in convoy for France, land that I loved.

Not that I knew much about France that amounted to anything: racy novels like Zola's *Nana,* hoary clichés about high life and worldly appetites, a beautiful and seductive language that I had valiantly studied in high school (to no good end), ravishing music by Ravel and Debussy, some of which I could actually play on the piano, and movies that seemed, in my provincial cave in hometown Baltimore, to cut close to the bone. I was a sucker for all that; it turned me into a Francophile (an amateur, however), and developed a taste in me—remnants of which still litter my psyche—for a touch of Gallic sophistication that I could call my own. And suddenly I was on my way to claim it at its source.

*Vive la France!* I said to myself as I threw up again on the first day out to sea. *Vive la gloire!*

We were all equally ignorant of France and the French in the Yankee Division. And the American Army was not about to fill the gaps in our education. It was not on their agenda. So we would have to take pot luck, just as we found it, and make our own judgments and our own mistakes. We would sail across the Atlantic, unthinking and blind, in the self-absorbed way of all traveling armies through history, and learn by doing, by being there. Nevertheless, it was still a kind of bliss. . . .

THE SS *Argentina* sailed from her Brooklyn berth at midnight on a Saturday in August 1944. It was ten weeks after D-Day. A band was playing somewhere under a shed at the end of the dock. I could hear the brass oom-pah and all the false cheer that went with it. My teeth were grinding together from the excitement. Word soon went out that Kate Smith was singing with the band, sentimental songs like "I'll Walk Alone," "I'll Be Seeing You," and "When the Moon Comes Over the Mountain," but none of us could hear her, if she was really there. We were too far away, way down at the other end of the dock. Besides, the embarkation noise, overall, was terrific; not much sound could rise above that. And, as we had been repeatedly warned, our sailing was supposed to be secret. I was sure all of Brooklyn could hear us.

"Who's singing?" Fedderman shouted.

"They say Kate Smith."

"The cornfields of kitsch!" he shouted again, leaving me blank-faced. I had never heard the word before. I had to ask him what it meant and how to spell it.

It was hours before we sailed, amid a tumult of misplaced bodies, lost gear, shouting officers, and frantic NCOs, some of whom were missing entire platoons. The decks of the *Argentina* were packed with exhausted GIs, sprawled out on their equipment, waiting to be allotted a hammock below deck. We had missed the evening meal and were chewing rations slowly to make them last; dry and gristly stuff, packed, it was claimed, with nutrients. They filled us up.

Bern stuck to my side and I to his. Fedderman, bulking large, also stayed close. (By now he had become totally dependent on Bern and me; it didn't matter that he was our prevailing intellectual and smartest kid, we had him on our hands.) I had the feeling that if Bern and I allowed ourselves to be separated, we would lose each other forever. (I worried less about Fedderman.) And it was easy to imagine: the *Argentina* was the largest ship I had ever seen. When we boarded, climbing the gangplank under our massive loads, I could see no end to her. She seemed to be without prow or stern, to go on forever. On our slow way up, I saw Bern suddenly stop and reach out with both arms, as though he wanted to embrace the *Argentina*'s black hull. He looked as though he was blessing the ship and maybe, as a superstitious infantryman, propitiating the gods at the same time.

By morning, the ship had made its first rendezvous a few miles off Cape Cod. About a dozen other ships—all shapes, all sizes—joined us there at dawn, gently rocking in a swelling surf. Watching them brought on our first seasickness, which we all took as a joke at first, especially when Fedderman chose to throw up into the wind. But we were all a little sick for the first twenty-four hours, and it wasn't long before the joke lost its point. It took Ralph Natale, one of our new men, another full day before he could sleep below deck.

Later in the afternoon, a second fleet joined us, one ship at a time. They slipped into position as though they had rehearsed it. By evening I could count sixty vessels—naval, cargo, troop transport, even a couple of aircraft carriers—spread in a stupendous 360-degree sweep that extended across the horizon. Standing on deck, immobilized by the power of what I saw, I could feel the strength of the SS *Argentina,* the ship's engines rumbling beneath my feet, the ship itself trembling with contained energy. Down below, the sea suddenly shifted. So did the position of the other ships. In the half-light of early evening, under a gauzy moon, the *Argentina* slowly rose and fell in a steady, repetitive movement.

"My God," Bern said, at the sight. He was standing alongside me on deck.

"It's beautiful," I said.

"One sub," Fedderman said. "That's all it would take." That was another way Fedderman liked to talk, as though it was his pleasure to scare us.

The next day we began to trace our zigzag route across the Atlantic. We could feel the strange, confusing motion as we changed direction, sometimes from hour to hour. Northeast by east, then northeast again, and back. By then the convoy had almost doubled in size, most of the ships traveling at the same speed, geared to the slowest. At the fringes, tough little destroyers moved at their own feisty speed, on the alert for a U-boat encounter. All was calm as we watched them.

. . .

EARLY that evening, I found Paul Willis standing on deck, staring out at the gray sea. From where we stood, we could hear the exhilarating whoosh of the *Argentina*'s wake. Even under restraint, the ship seemed to move fast.

"Some sight," I remember saying, feeling a little shy. I was still not used to talking to Willis.

"Yeah."

"I never imagined anything like this," I went on.

Willis looked me in the eye, something he rarely did. He seemed to be trying to make up his mind whether to speak or not. Finally, he spit into the Atlantic and asked, "Is Fedderman going to make it? In your educated opinion?"

"What do you mean?"

"Has he got it? Can we trust him? Will he be there? He's your pal, you should know."

I had been asking myself those questions for a couple of weeks, and the answers made me unhappy. "As much as anybody, I guess" was what I said. But I spoke without conviction. Certainly as much as you, I wanted to add.

"I've made a recommendation to Rocky," Willis then said, sounding self-important.

"What kind of recommendation?"

"Put Johnson at the head of the BAR, with you and Keaton as assists. Look for another scout to replace Johnson. Maybe that new man, Brewster. Brewster has an eagle eye, ever notice? Keep Fedderman an ordinary squad member, with Natale. With no special duties. That's the part that counts, no special duties."

He had certainly thought it through. I said nothing.

"I think it's going to happen, too." Willis puffed up as he spoke. "Rocky likes it. We're going to have to carry Fedderman. Maybe Natale, too. I know the handwriting when I see it."

I didn't answer. I didn't really want to talk to Paul Willis about Ira Fedderman. It was disloyal. Besides, Willis was right; we *were* going to have to carry Fedderman, and I didn't want to be identified with that.

For a moment or two, Willis and I watched the ghostly green spume, the phosphorescent gleam, trailing us. It was vaguely unsettling, as though a whole sinister other life was festering underwater, beneath our very feet. That feeling grew stronger as Willis and I watched together.

An omen?

"We need harmony in the squad, you know," Willis said, looking at me again. "For what we're going to."

Harmony, indeed—at the very least. I nodded in agreement; I would give Willis that. Then, apparently satisfied with our exchange, he turned to look at the convoy. I could see him taking it in, from one end to the other. In a moment, he braced himself as though he was coming to attention. His eyes opened wide. I saw wonder, amazement, awe on his dim, pale face as he looked out to sea.

My God, I thought, Willis lives! Look at him!

No question about it, at that moment, my feelings about him changed. Willis became real to me at last. He was no longer just the thieving freak, the first squad's feckless punk.

MOSTLY we lived on board the *Argentina* by comforting routine: sleeping in hammocks that rose six-high from floor to ceiling; jammed into cabins, public rooms, the hold (Antonovich and Gallagher slept on another deck with the other officers, higher up; we never saw them); taking our meals quickly on our feet, standing at a chest-high mess table that was bolted to the floor; lining up for the washbasins and toilets in the head, where we could throw up; then on deck for the rest of the day (and the night if it suited), where we could throw up into the sea; participating in lifeboat drill, while the NCOs, frustrated at our indifference, threw tantrums; gambling (poker and dice); talking, mostly rumors and sex or rumors about sex, with Barney Barnato, who was strangely subdued during the crossing, relating vague anecdotes to the rest of the platoon about his colored past; napping often; reading.

I read a lot, my habit, mostly tough little genre mysteries by Chandler and Hammett, but more serious stuff, too—a novel by Lion Feuchtwanger, for one, called *Success* (remembered from my parents' library). The high-minded Central European aura of this book, its obsession with justice, has stayed with me all these years; the novel still sits on my bookshelf. I was susceptible to moral issues then, powerfully so, and still am. I believed in the universal struggle between good and evil. Innocent and guilty. Right and wrong. In choices and in "us and them." That was how I saw the world: in simple, direct adolescent terms, for I was still an adolescent. That was why it was easy for me to hate the enemy.

Keaton and Fedderman also read, as much as I did, Ira maybe even more, and so did many other GIs aboard the *Argentina*; we were not exceptional. The ship carried the entire paperback Armed Services Library, for us an indispensable resource. Every time the SS *Argentina* crossed the Atlantic from the States, it unloaded another well-read division in the ETO.

At sea, during those dreamy days of late August, we had no responsibilities. All that was demanded of us was that we behave ourselves. I felt this trust implicitly, and I think everyone else did, too. There were almost no dramatic incidents, no disturbances aboard ship. Harmony, Willis had called for during our unexpected little exchange; and we had it, with almost no perceptible strain. We were suspended in time and watery space, headed for a mysterious destination. We may have been caged on our ship, but it still represented a kind of freedom to most of us. I never wanted the crossing to end. I was willing to sail on to the end of the world in order to hold on to that serenity.

But, of course, one morning ten days later we awoke to see a coastline. Green hills, modest cliffs, white beaches slowly came into view; an unexpected prospect. It was France, we were told, Normandy itself, close to the great bloody battlefields of D-Day. An electric hush fell over the ship as it began to slow.

Bern and Ira and I stood together on deck, gazing in silence at the Old World, powerfully resisting the idea of landfall. Just beyond landfall our whole future lay in wait. In the far distance, we could make out a small church with a squat stone tower, then some ugly pillboxes positioned atop a hillside, and finally a lone person, wearing blue coveralls, bicycling along a road that paralleled the shore. The bicycle looked as if it was barely moving. It was a first taste of Europe, never to be repeated, and I found it strangely moving.

The *Argentina* crept in a foot at a time. Overhead the gulls wheeled and stayed close. Fedderman, suddenly jittery, began to tell terrible jokes, until Bern told him to shut up. Directly ahead lay Cherbourg, the old Norman city, the great port now preparing to welcome the Yankee Division. The rest of the convoy, we discovered, had peeled off overnight into smaller clusters, most of them heading for the United Kingdom, for Plymouth and Southampton and other ports. Operations in Cherbourg were still not normal more than two months after D-Day. Half the port was wrecked, the rest was barely functioning. Cherbourg could not yet dock a ship the size of the SS *Argentina*.

We began to gather, lining up on deck with all our equipment, shifting irritably from one foot to another, suffering nerves and stomachaches and impatience, the soldier's oldest enemies. Behind us stood mounds of duffel bags, stuffed with all our personal possessions, including illicit goods, too, like whiskey and gin. Arch was striding back and forth in front of us, his eyes bulging like a predatory fish's. He examined us, muttering under his breath. He checked our clothes, our equipment, whether we were clean-shaven. Did we pass muster? Were we okay? There was no comment, merely a nervous twitching, peculiar to Arch, back and forth. Behind Arch, Lieutenant Gallagher sauntered along, as though he didn't know what to do with himself, his small-boned face almost lost in the depths of his helmet. He had a nice sunburn, and so did Captain Antonovich, from a pleasant ocean crossing on an open deck that was off-limits to the rest of us.

An hour passed. My back straps hurt; I loosened them. Alongside me, Fedderman was groaning quietly. It was a habit of his, a way of expressing anxiety. He had others, like clicking his teeth, very loud. Now his pack rested on his fat butt, way too low, and his ammo belt was down near his groin. You couldn't get near him without getting bruised by a piece of misplaced equipment. The saddest sack of all, as he had come to be marked by everyone in Company C. (Maybe Rocky thought he could salvage Fedderman when he agreed to take him into the squad. That was certainly possible; Rocky seemed to be attracted to the idea of redemption in others.)

It made me feel contemptuous, Fedderman's sloppiness, his incompetence, his seeming lack of pride. Why didn't he care more? I wasn't much more competent at rolling a full-field pack, I could be a slob, too, but I cared and I tried and so did Bern Keaton. (Oh, how we cared; that part of us must have been insufferable to Fedderman.)

On the other side of Fedderman, Bern stood at rest, unusually calm, it seemed to me, for what was going on all around us. He was engrossed in *Of Mice and Men*. We all had books with us, stolen from the ship's library. Fedderman was carrying Zane Grey's *Riders of the Purple Sage* (he claimed to love Westerns, had a whole theory about their unacknowledged aesthetic value in the canon of American literature), and I had a copy of *The Pocket Book of Verse* stuffed into one fatigue pocket and Harry Kurnitz's smart little mystery, *Fast Company*, in the other. I could still tell you the plot.

Down below, the engines suddenly stopped. A vast silence spread everywhere. Between the *Argentina* and the city of Cherbourg lay an expanse of choppy water, perhaps three hundred yards in all to shore. A stiff wind had begun to blow. Clouds were moving fast to the east, into the Norman countryside. Another half-hour passed. It grew chilly on deck and suddenly we realized that our officers had disappeared. Then Fedderman's teeth began to click; a horrible, foreboding sound.

"Okay, men, this is how we're going in." It was Arch, finally ready with our orders. "Pay attention. All of you." He sounded oddly subdued, almost schoolmasterish, which was not Arch's style. We could hardly hear him.

We were going in on Higgins boats, he told us, landing craft that had carried the infantry ashore on D-Day. He paused a moment, while we assimilated this. We would board the boats by descending the steep sides of the *Argentina*'s hull on a rope ladder that was being lowered in front of us at the very moment that Arch was describing it. I swallowed a momentary panic when I saw the crew at work, then began to focus on the problem itself, which of course was a familiar one. But there was no escape for me today, no KP or latrine duty to volunteer for. That was clear. This time, for the first time, I was going down the ladder with everyone else. Right. So be it. Amen. I glanced over at Bern. He had put his book away. I thought he was smirking a little. As I've said, Bern was good at rope ladders.

"We're going to have to take him down with us," he said, in a calm voice.

"Who?"

Bern nodded at Fedderman, who stood between us making a lot of noise, hyperventilating. He seemed to be blind to us he was so scared. Maybe, I thought, if I concentrated on Fedderman, I could forget myself. That kind of displacement had worked for me before, in other situations.

"You guys make a move without me, I'll crush you," Fedderman said, between his teeth. He took in a couple of loud breaths. His moon face stared straight ahead. His rifle was dirty and he was beginning to lose things from his pack. A can of C rations fell out, bouncing on the deck. He was still hyperventilating, heaving away between Bern and me. To hell with him, I thought, looking away. I hated helplessness in others; it was too close to home.

And yet, in another twenty minutes, during which Bern and I put Fedderman together, stuffed his pack, hoisted it higher, tightened the straps, and pulled his belt up, we began the descent, along with fourteen thousand others. Of our group, Rocky went first, disappearing over the side of the ship like a silent wraith, which was how he had behaved all the way across the Atlantic, holding tight to himself for the entire journey. Willis and Johnson followed, Johnson carrying the BAR (Willis had won his point with Rocky). Ralph Natale and George Brewster followed them, also silent and grim. Then Barney Barnato lifted himself over the rail, pink-cheeked and flabby; as he disappeared over the side, he was grinning in a silly way, as though he had known this was coming all along.

Bern and I flanked Ira Fedderman even closer, gripping him by each arm, as he finally got himself over the railing and slowly positioned himself on the top rung of the ladder. He was shivering. So was I.

"Keep moving and don't look down," Bern ordered, and we started, our feet testing each rung, paced by those platoon members who were below us; we were crooning into Fedderman's ear at every step.

"One foot at a time, old boy. Don't rush it." That was Bern.

"Don't open your eyes. We've got you." Me, lying.

"Not too fast now, you'll step on Barney." Bern again.

"Jesus, Ira."

"Sweet mother of God."

Minutes passed. An hour. All of eternity, it seemed. Then somehow, while the ladder slapped hard against the *Argentina's* hull, we were at the bottom, or close enough. Men clustered like flies to the side of the ship on our right and left, jumping one at a time onto pontoon bridges that had been laid down, then into the clumsy vessels waiting alongside them. We jumped too, Bern first, then Fedderman, then me. One by one, knees buckling, we crashed on deck. A moment later, up near the prow of the Higgins boat, Fedderman stood alongside me, panting. His nose was bleeding. "For God's sake, wipe your nose," I ordered irritably. Fedderman looked startled but did as he was told. Then, as the vessel began to fill, Bern lighted a cigarette, hiding it in the palm of his hand, while Fedderman poked at his nose with his handkerchief, examining the bloodstains with a resentful look.

So you finally made it down the ladder, I remember saying to myself; you actually did it. The taste of that was sweet.

But we weren't in Cherbourg yet.

Finally loaded, the boat headed for shore. A couple of hundred yards farther on, it began to slow, then suddenly came to a halt alongside a dozen others, each one jammed tight with troops, like ours. A couple of minutes passed. I could feel Fedderman's massive presence behind me. The butt of his rifle slapped against my thigh, and Bern's canteen—or Willis's, I'm not sure—began to rub against my hipbone, creating a maddening pressure. Up ahead I could see square granite houses, with their shutters drawn. There were also a couple of shuttered depots and what looked like a half-empty market, with empty crates piled in the middle of the street. A few bicycles rolled by, their riders glancing at us. Everything was out of scale, disproportionately small. The strange weight of foreignness was everywhere we looked.

Then the prow of the landing craft slowly opened; we drifted in a few more feet and stopped again, rocking in the surf.

"Holy shit," Rocky said, eyeing the water that lapped at our feet.

"Okay, men," Lieutenant Gallagher said, addressing us from the top of an oil barrel. Where had he come from? "This is the end of the line for you guys. Or maybe the beginning." He paused a moment to laugh at his little joke, but he laughed alone; no one was in the mood for little jokes. "What you do now," he went on, suddenly looking serious, "is head for those steps there." He pointed to some stone steps cut into the side of a quay many yards off. "It's all shallow waterfront from here on. You'll find trucks waiting there for the platoon. Look for your squad leader. Stick with your buddies. Keep it orderly and keep it moving. And no business with civilians. I mean no business. Of any kind."

I could hardly see Gallagher's face as he spoke, lost as it was inside his helmet. Absolutely nothing of government issue fit him.

Then we were off, scrambling up to our chests into the dirty gray water, holding our rifles horizontally over our heads to keep them dry, sludging along step-by-step toward Cherbourg. For every one of us, I'm sure, making it across the fifty or so yards that remained was like trying to walk through water in our most dire dreams; our thighs ached painfully and our hearts pounded double-time from the struggle to break through.

But we did break through minutes later, yelling with relief as we scrambled up the steps of the quay to the street. Soaking, we quickly managed to board one of the trucks waiting there, under Arch's nervous eye. Bern and I hoisted ourselves up, shoving Fedderman's stubborn wet butt ahead of us to give him some extra leverage. Then, just as we began to settle down, we had to do it all over again, because it turned out that we were on the wrong truck. Everybody was on the wrong truck.

"How about it, Arch," Rocky complained as we milled around in the street, complaining too.

Finally, along with everyone else in the third platoon, we were pointed in the right direction and boarded the correct vehicles efficiently. The roll call proceeded: "Johnson (Yo!), Willis (Here!), Barnato (*Ja!*), Natale (Yo!), Brewster (Yo!), Keaton (Ho!), Fedderman . . . Fedderman . . ." then a third time, "Fedderman (*Ici!*), Kotlowitz (Here!)" By then, we were seated along the insides of the truck, facing each other, our teeth on edge.

Someone noticed that Arch had succeeded in remaining perfectly dry while getting ashore. We all wondered about that, muttering under our breath. "He probably flew the fuck in," Fedderman said, smiling in that sarcastic way of his, but he echoed our feelings exactly. We all knew how inventive our master sergeant could be when it came to his own creature comforts.

In another moment, the second squad arrived, rowdy as always. They clambered into the truck, yelling and stepping all over our feet. (There were no sad sacks in the second squad since Fedderman's departure, no sissies.) We sat quietly. While they were rowdy we would get some rest. Let them yell and carry on.

The trucks began to rev up, then idle, then rev again. Half the squad was already asleep. Then at last we were rolling, once again part of a convoy. Cherbourg, I thought, straining to see the city. It looked different, it smelled different. Yeasty and pungent and alien—but indisputably French. Overhead, the gulls were still with us. I watched them trying to keep pace, circling in formation, then swooping independently from one truck to another. They seemed to be in better order than we were. What a noise we made, what an engine roar! My eyes began to close. Sleep moved in, but first I wanted to reach out and embrace the strange city that lay around us and, like a fool, shout, "I'm here!" *Me voici!* But it was too late for that. My attenuated French had vanished with the day's struggles. I was already half-dead to the world.

# FOUR

# Short-Arms

WE SOON learned that Antonovich liked to talk about Kansas and Nebraska, where he had triumphed at football, and by implication about the whole Midwest and its dependencies; and with so much time on our hands in Normandy, so much waiting time, he had all the opportunities he needed.

In theory, he was supposed to be lecturing C Company on infantry tactics (there was really no other subject in the YD), but after completing basic training and Tennessee maneuvers, as well as two months at Camp Jackson refining details before we shipped overseas, there was not much left—in the abstract, at least—to learn about infantry tactics. We knew it all, was the general attitude in the Yankee Division; all that was left was to apply what we knew.

Gradually then, Antonovich's daily class, held right after the midday meal within the cramped apple orchard in which C Company was bivouacked, began to drift in other directions, according to Antonovich's whim, and before long we were engaged by an intellectual syllabus that might have been entitled The Great American Plains and Their Incomparable Metropoli, most particularly the cities of Omaha, Kansas City (the wrong one), and Abilene, glorious gateways to the glorious west. Those were Michael Antonovich's favorite towns, his American urban lodestones, the homes of the really free and the truly truly brave.

Of course it was absurd, the whole idea of Michael Antonovich lecturing us about anything. (How he chewed away, bite by bite, at the substance of that beefy geography while we struggled to stay awake after the midday meal in the late summer heat.) We all knew that we were waiting at that moment for orders to join the new Ninth Army, which was slowly being formed with fastidious care under the command of General Simpson, whose name we had never heard before. Nobody tried to keep our situation secret. It was probably common knowledge all over the ETO, on both sides of the lines, American and German. Several other divisions were also waiting on the Normandy peninsula, as we were, camped in a patient cluster near the sea. We had already been there two weeks, living a privileged life. The word was that the Ninth Army, when its time came, would join the Allied forces somewhere in northern France, near the Belgian border. (*"Ro-ses are smiling in Pi-car-dy,"* I sang to myself as the rumor spread; it was a sentimental old tune from World War I that my father had become attached to during his own Army days overseas, and it had stuck to me through childhood like a birthmark.) The cities of Lille, Amiens, and Roubaix were mentioned. So was the Ardennes.

It could take months to put a new Army together, while we waited for fresh divisions to arrive from the UK and the States, and nearly as long to get it into action. So there was no hurry. That was what Lieutenant Gallagher told us—more, certainly, than he should have—and it was what we wanted to believe. Waiting: that suited us fine. We lived in a kind of trance-like state, camped in the midst of heady calvados country, near the village of Montebourg, hidden from the road by thick hedgerows, and always a little high from the pungent smell of rotting apples and smoky wood fires that never quite burned out. It was a classic bivouac camp, perfect in almost every detail. Even our mail reached us soon after we arrived, bringing on a sudden rush of nostalgia. Did we deserve such bounty? We didn't ask. It was enough to know that once again the war was somewhere else and good luck to it.

But in the meantime, while we waited, what were they to do with us?

While Michael Antonovich lectured C Company on the glories of the great American Middle West, Lieutenant Gallagher decided to offer a series of talks on battles that had changed the world—on the theory, I imagine, that such a course might fire us with a certain zeal for action. But it soon became clear that Gallagher was a total dilettante, at best an ambitious novice on the subject, and always shaky when it came to essential details. Nobody cared. As usual, Gallagher had the right spirit; he knew how to force his ideas on us without stirring resentment. Marathon, Thermopylae, then (a great gap) Lexington, Waterloo, Gettysburg, and the Marne, which was Gallagher's favorite, especially the part about how the taxis of Paris had helped to save the city—one detail, at least, that he got right.

In Gallagher's lectures, every battle soon began to
sound exactly like every other, in the general mess of
skewed facts, except for the names of the battlefields
themselves. Marathon and the Marne, Lexington and
Waterloo, they were all one. So were hoplites, redcoats,
minutemen, Johnny Rebs, Tommies, and poilus. From his
training at OCS, apparently, Gallagher had retained an
ideal of Battle, a pure abstraction that served for all battles, and through his bright and disorganized monologues,
which followed Antonovich's on the afternoon schedule,
he tried to impose that ideal on the troops of C Company.
It was Ira Fedderman who developed this theory for Bern
and me—one of his plummier perceptions, I thought.

Yes, it was absurd, as absurd as Antonovich's meander-
ings through the Middle West. We knew it and I hope Gallagher knew it. Yet, despite really ghastly boredom, we
stuck loyally to our platoon leader and pretended to be
enthralled by his talks. In that way, we proved to ourselves
that we loved him. Time had to be killed while the new
Ninth Army slowly took shape, and if absurdity would help
to hurry the process . . . well, we could put up with a little
absurdity.

Antonovich and Gallagher were really talking to dead-
weights after the midday break. Sprawled out on the
sweet-smelling ground, a litter of loose Yankee bones at
their ease, the third platoon and the rest of the company
languished inattentively in front of their commanding officers, trying hard to stay awake. We faked it for Gallagher,
nodded off for Antonovich. Every now and then, Master
Sergeant Archambault would step lightly through the
sprawl and prod our stuffed bodies with a stick if we fell
asleep. "Stop that dreaming," he would mutter dutifully,

but we could tell his mind was elsewhere; he could hardly keep from yawning himself.

Midday meals were huge: meat and poultry requisitioned from Cherbourg depots, Norman potatoes, in theory off-limits; breads baked by our own cooks, in their element at last; steaming gravy that took half a day to digest. It all sat heavy and killed our energy. Up front, facing this postprandial trance and in no hurry to finish, Antonovich talked on about Omaha or Kansas City and trains and beef and the connections among all three, about wheat futures, cattle prices, the humane slaughter of edible beasts, and so on, including an occasional obvious fact about dealing with life on the great prairies in the midst of a hard winter. For example, always wear a hat in freezing weather, he told us, because body heat escapes through the head. Things like that—totally irrelevant and all promptly forgotten.

Meanwhile, Gallagher was at us about frontal assaults, flanking operations, guerrilla tactics, and the special military skill of the Huns. That was what he called the Germans in his battle recitations, the Huns, as though the YD was still at St.-Mihiel or Belleau Wood. I don't think Gallagher was thrilled by the subject. I think he just stumbled on it when he realized how much time had to be filled while we waited for the Ninth Army to grow to full strength. I also think that he made up everything as he went along; he was always a great improviser. So we yawned, dozed, snored, and pretended to care. Meanwhile the sun shone, apples fell from the trees, every morning we hiked five to ten miles on mostly deserted roads, and we were bewitched.

.   .   .

ARCH, who loved the weapon and insisted on its primacy, put us through bayonet drill for a half-hour every day.

"Fix bayonets!" he would shout, and we did, far too slowly for Arch's approval, our hands trembling as we fumbled with the scabbard and blade in a shaky attempt to fix it to the muzzles of our rifles without drawing blood. We were scared of the bayonet. It carried a terrible power. It could disembowel a man. Would we ever have to use it? Could I disembowel a man? I doubted it.

Then, swallowing our fear and following Arch's orders, we aimed, thrust, slashed, or whichever—screaming "Kill! Kill!" in our thin teen-age voices—Bern and Ira and I. Self-consciousness overwhelmed us. Squeaky sounds came from our throats. We could hear them. "Keel, Keel!" Ira tried to yell, in a threatening falsetto, as though he were some kind of Latin movie villain.

Arch, looking disgusted, kept us at it, over and over again with no breaks, his own voice choking with pretended passion. "Girls, girls!" he shouted, only half-joking. I lunged for Fedderman (thrown totally off-balance, as I always was when carrying that huge knife at the end of my rifle). Bern went for Willis, Brewster for Natale, while Johnson and Barnato ran at each other, in a manner of speaking, both of them a little too serious, too ardent, I thought, and clumsy. Their unsheathed bayonets actually touched each other's flesh at one point, breaking a strict taboo. "Watch it, shitheads!" Arch screamed. "That's real skin and blood there." From the sidelines, Rocky observed the action in silence and bit into an apple. He looked serious. God knows what he was thinking.

Another half-hour a day was spent on weapon-cleaning, which we performed by now with near-perfect skill and

speed. (We had certainly practiced it enough.) Even Fedderman and I were near-perfect at it, stripping our rifles
with our eyes closed, then minutes later putting the rifles
together again, piece by irreplaceable piece. We loved to
do that (at last), showing off for each other, just as we
loved our M-1s, without exception. We fondled them,
stroked them, sometimes held them in our arms and
hugged them while we slept. It was another kind of propi-
tiation. I knew men who used to kiss their rifles surrepti-
tiously. Paul Willis was one of them.

We could even take apart the BAR, although with less
confidence and no love. With the BAR we might fumble a
bit, look confused, hesitate, but in the end the job was
done. But when, I sometimes wondered, would we ever
find ourselves in a combat situation in which we would
have the time and the opportunity to strip our weapons
and fastidiously clean each piece? I knew, and everyone
else knew, that in combat we would have to depend on
pouring oil down the gun barrels and slopping the trigger
mechanisms and the stock in the same way, at top speed.
But then we were not being serious in our Norman
orchard; we knew that we were merely killing time while
we waited for orders from General Simpson.

So we hiked, had bayonet practice, listened to absurd
lectures, cleaned our weapons, ate enormous unhealthy
meals, and kept house in our pup tents, which were rigor-
ously inspected every morning after breakfast. Sometimes
Arch looked in, holding his nose as a joke, other times Gallagher showed up, and even, once or twice, Antonovich
himself. Mostly, though, it was Rocky's job, as squad
leader, and I have to say for him that he didn't take it
lightly. I think that inspection appealed to his sense of

order and pride, and for Rocky most of us tried to keep our nests fastidious.

Maybe it was a good thing that Bern had moved in with Roger Johnson, who now headed the BAR team, while I took on Fedderman shortly after we landed in Normandy. This was not done casually. It happened only after Bern and I shared a couple of serious, even mournful exchanges about how our individual failings seemed to feed the other's, so that it would probably be a sound idea to separate, if only temporarily. The whole painful discussion was accompanied by a lot of symbolic bowing and scraping and calculated politesse on behalf of our tender feelings for each other. But it worked and the deal was set: Fedderman and Johnson did not object, neither did Rocky.

At least with Fedderman I could complain as much as I wanted, berating him about his sloppiness and general disorder without feeling guilty. He was worse than sloppy: his side of the tent was a litter, far messier than anything Bern and I had ever produced in our time; mine of course was now perfect, for Rocky's sake. Soon my complaints turned into the kind of relentless nagging that kills the spirit without fail. Then I discovered that I was actually beginning to enjoy it—the nagging, that is. Naturally, this disturbed my sense of myself.

Sharing a pup tent could do that to you. It put you in someone else's thrall. It forced you into someone else's domestic embrace. Suddenly you turned over part of your world, perhaps the essential part, to a stranger, an intruder—in Fedderman's case bulky, twitchy, high-strung, and incompetent—with noises, habits, and intimate smells of his own; and he returned the favor. (It was hard enough to get used to your own smells, much less someone else's.) Men were not made to live together, I was learning for a second time. It created a false situation, bound by unyielding tension. I would not forget that lesson. It would last for years.

So I nagged Fedderman, pressed him hard—too hard, perhaps—telling myself that I was protecting my identity by proclaiming my integrity. Nothing helped. I think Fedderman was probably too self-absorbed to care about my proclamations and maybe immune by then to such assaults, which had probably been going on since he was a child. He had certainly made sure to grow a very thick skin, or appear to.


THEN, one day, some damn fool from A Company stepped out of line on a morning's march, just a couple of yards onto the beach that ran alongside the road we were hiking on. Apparently he wanted to pee, despite all the signs that still littered the sand like tombstones: "*Minen,*" "*Achtung,*" "*Verboten,*" all illustrated with vivid pictures of skulls and crossbones. His misstep triggered a German mine that took off his foot. That misadventure caused a flurry of nervous daytime lectures on the dangers that still lay in wait in Normandy for unwary infantrymen. Antonovich lectured us, Gallagher, even Rocky. The war was still real. You could get killed in paradise, too. We never even bothered to learn the victim's name.

And the French, where were they? Out of bounds. Off-limits. Not to be spoken to, not to be approached or touched, as though they, and not the Germans, were the real enemy. This hurt. What were we doing in France if not to liberate the population from the shame of humiliating defeat and once again make the French-American alliance strong? But this was a question only I seemed to ask. No one else apparently gave it a thought. I was alone in the third platoon as a Francophile.

We were bivouacked between two small towns that maintained a closely linked existence, and communication was brisk between them. A steady bicycle traffic, moving in both directions, rolled along the road that bordered our orchard. We could catch a glimpse over the tops of our hedgerow from time to time of farmers driving an occasional vehicle, probably burning black-market Yankee gasoline, carrying a load of skimpy produce from one village to the other. I could hear conversations, too, fragments of the real thing, a sharp provincial French that was spoken at such speed that I could barely make a word out here and there.

But we could only look. Somehow the authorities—American? French? I never knew—had decided to keep us apart. Was it the fear that we might be infected by political ideas that would subvert our manly valor? Was it the possibility of catching a venereal disease, which we had been obsessively educated about from the day we entered the Army? Or was it just to save everyone from the sort of unpredictable trouble that often erupts when two people who are without a common language meet as occupier and occupied? Probably a bit of all three, and I resented it.

But the regulations didn't always work. Accidental meetings took place. Unexpected confrontations happened. We were all witness to them, mostly on our morning hikes where contact was unavoidable. One morning, for example, heading along a dirt road that ran through the back countryside, loping dreamily along, we passed a small stone house set a couple of feet back from the road. There were no other houses nearby; it was perfectly isolated and perfectly ordinary. (That morning we were just the third platoon, swinging along under Lieutenant Gallagher's easy direction, enjoying the sharp saline smell that swept in from the coast with the morning fog.) The house, which seemed to speak precisely of Normandy, was shaded by an enormous ancient fruit tree. A sweet glimpse, I thought, of the true pastoral France.

We slowed down as we stepped by; everyone wanted a look, I guess. I saw a small child, a girl maybe three years old, standing in the open doorway of the house, dressed in a blue peasant smock. She was sucking her thumb and gazing at her feet shyly, pretending not to see us. *"Bonjour!"* I shouted, happy to be actually speaking French. Almost instantly, at my greeting, a hand reached through the doorway, grabbed the child by the shoulder, and pulled her inside. Then an angry wizened face, an old woman's furious face, glowered at us a moment from the door, and disappeared. What was that, I wondered? We marched on, Gallagher suddenly giving the count in a loud voice. I looked back, hoping to see more, still wondering, but there was nothing, only an empty doorway and a giant fruit tree shading an old stone house.

The experience was repeated a few days later, with a single variation. As we neared the house a second time, the child seemed to be waiting for us in the doorway, still sucking her thumb, still gazing at her feet. Once again, she was wearing her blue smock. This morning I did not shout a greeting. Nevertheless, as we passed, the child was again pulled inside the house, this time by a young woman wearing overalls and wooden shoes, and with a scarf covering her head.

Before she disappeared, the young woman took a moment to stare at us. I saw her lips move as she said something to the child. Or to us, it was hard to tell. Then we were on our way again, Gallagher picking up the count in a loud voice, as he had the first time, moving along fast, as though he wanted to put the scene behind us.

Of course, I began to think about the two women and the child, vague thoughts that never really came into focus, and I guess others did, too. But, in fact, none of us found the incident important enough to mention. By afternoon, we were back to bayonet practice and silly lectures.

It happened only once again. This time, perhaps a week later, Gallagher decided that the platoon would take a break in the field that adjoined the stone house. There was plenty of room, no trees, level ground. Even so, I found this decision a little strange, as though Gallagher was asking for trouble, as though he wanted to precipitate some action, something he had an instinct for at times. We headed for the field, sprawled out back-to-back as we always did, lazed, and smoked. There was a certain amount of easy chatter, I remember; we were still cheerful at that time. In a moment or two, while we rested there, the old woman, the ancient crone we had seen the first day, appeared from the house. She stood at the edge of the field, shaking her fist in the air and declaiming at us. It was a kind of outraged keen, filled with incomprehensible words, both bitter-sounding and threatening.

The platoon was embarrassed. We stirred uncomfortably and tried to look away. It was clear to everyone that we were probably trespassing on the old woman's property, that we had invaded her privacy. While she shouted at us, the child appeared at her side. She was wearing the same blue smock and was still unsmiling. Behind them, in a window of the house, we caught a glimpse of the young woman, the one we had seen a week before, hiding in the shadows. Today she was not wearing a scarf over her head. She was bareheaded, and bald.

"Jesus, did you see that?" Fedderman cried out. For once, he lost his blasé air.

"On your feet, men," Gallagher ordered, turning his back on the old woman and the house.

"What was it?" Bern asked.

Willis and Johnson and Natale were staring at the house. Barney Barnato looked cynical. Rocky was lining us up, one by one, as though we were still in basic training, urging us to move fast. The other squads were already on the road. Then the child began to cry as the old woman shoved her toward the house. I could see her pinching the child's shoulders. We saw the young woman again in the same window, a moment's glimpse of a nearly bare skull, with a faint, thin fuzz sprouting from it.

"What was it?" Bern asked again, looking back.

But we were already on our way and Gallagher was trying to get us to sing. (Another lost cause.) "Fedderman," Bern pleaded.

"She's a collaborator!" Ira shouted, over his shoulder. He was excited. "She slept with the Germans. You can tell from her hair. That's what the French do to collaborators, shave their heads. She's a collaborator whore."

We marched on through the suddenly sour air. Nobody spoke. I could tell that Bern was mulling it over. So was I.

Bern had his Catholic judgmental face on, disapproval and disappointment all over it, and I was sure I looked the same. Our moral balance had been upset. Ambiguities suddenly shaded the Normandy landscape.

How could Fedderman be so sure that the woman was a whore? What did he know about collaboration? He was assuming too much, as always. Maybe she was just a (slightly stupid) peasant girl who had fallen in love with *ein deutsch Soldat* (also slightly stupid) who happened to be stationed in the area . . . at a time when it was easy to fall in love. Suppose, in fact, that she had been raped by a German soldier or that someone with a grudge had informed against her, or any one of many other possibilities, all of which seemed plausible to me.

And what about the child? Vengeance is mine, saith the Lord (at his worst), but surely the child was an innocent. I had never before thought of French collaboration with the Germans in such immediate, human terms. The truth was that I had never thought of French collaboration in any terms. Probably the idea was too painful to consider. I would have to pay closer attention, start to ponder a little, try to keep my expectations from fogging the truth.

It was life close to the bone, I told myself.


ONCE again, our world was changing. The witching hour was approaching. We began to wake up, as though an alarm had been sounded. Had the Ninth Army finally reached full strength? Were all the fresh divisions in place, eager for action, ready to move to Lille, Amiens, or Roubaix? (I had never heard of Roubaix.) No one was talking this time. Gallagher was keeping his mouth shut. The subject was off-limits. This made it even more real, more foreboding. *Ro-ses are smi-ling in Pi-car-dy* . . .

Daily training became serious again. (It was hard for me not to link this childishly with the dark fate of the bald young woman in the stone house, as though she had hexed us, as though we needed hexing.) Antonovich's and Gallagher's lectures ended. Guard duty was rotated by the numbers, in strict fashion. All other duties were handled in the same rigorous way. There was a company forced march every other day (no more sweet little five-mile trots at our own pace)—led by Antonovich, who was seriously out of shape after weeks in the Normandy countryside—with weapons, ammo, and full-field packs, twenty to twenty-five miles at top speed, and barely a break at the end of each hour. Every forced march was like another small death for each of us, but especially for Ira Fedderman.

It damn near broke my heart one morning to see Fedderman struggling in front of me at about the fifth mile of a twenty-mile march. His fat, squat thighs were desperately pumping away as we raced along. Every few seconds, an asthmatic wheeze cut his breath like splinters of glass, while bits and pieces of equipment fell out of his pack as it slid lower and lower onto his powerful haunches. He still couldn't roll a decent pack, despite my hectoring.

At the end of another mile, barely ten minutes later, Fedderman stumbled once, held on a moment, and cried out in a weak voice. Then he went down on his knees before collapsing flat out into a massive heap. I could hear him struggling for breath as I stepped over him; by then I was also struggling for breath.

"Keep going, men," Rocky called out, calmly moving out of line to stand alongside Fedderman. "Eyes ahead."

A few minutes later, as we stumbled along, Fedderman passed us stretched out in the back of a jeep that always followed the company on forced marches for just such emergencies. I could see that he was weeping quietly. I didn't want to be a witness to that. I had never seen Fedderman cry. I had never seen anyone in the first squad cry. We all looked away, Rocky biting his lips with bitter regret, I'm sure. It was a demoralizing sight. It was terrible.

IT MUST have been intolerable for Fedderman to fail like that, almost as a way of life. In the days that followed, it seemed to me, his emotional temperature dropped; the Fedderman fires, which always burned so intensely, had been tamped down by too many misadventures. I felt it most strongly inside our tent at night, while he slept his vulnerable sleep alongside me, snoring his heavy snores, the raspy snores of an asthmatic, dreaming his (undoubtedly) bad dreams. We never spoke about his collapse. I pretended that it had never happened. Fedderman, however, somehow made it through the next march, and the next—last man in the company column, a hundred yards behind the rest of us. But he made it. We never spoke about that either. I left him strictly alone, as we all did, and after that I stopped nagging him. Let him be a slob, I thought. Let him be whatever he had to be.

AS LIFE began to change, the first squad changed with it. Some of our efficiency unraveled, and with it our sense of our own capabilities—all hard-won at Camp Jackson and later and not an easy loss for an infantry unit to accept.

(This must have been happening throughout the YD, as tension spiraled and rumors about the future spread.) Rocky's authority lost just a bit of its luster, and there were breaches of conduct and trust among the squad members, sometimes expressed in unexpected aberrant conversations.

Late one night, for example, as we shared guard duty in the damp chill that had come over Normandy in early fall, Barney Barnato sidled up to me in the dark and put his mouth close to my ear. "Kid," he said. Just like that. As though we were old pals. I pulled away. Like Bern, I preferred not to get too close to Barney. I always kept my distance. I was afraid he might get stuck to me for life if I came too close.

"You're nervous," Barney said, in a whisper. "I can feel it. You shouldn't be nervous with me. It's only Barney." It was two o'clock in the morning, the sky was streaked with the potent light of constellations that seemed to be a mere five feet away. Reach out and you could almost touch them. "It's cold," Barney said.

"Yes, it is."

"Don't be afraid," Barney said. "You're not a child anymore. There's nothing to be afraid of."

I knew what was coming. (It had been worrying me ever since Barney got back from his emergency furlough after maneuvers; it had been worrying Bern, too, who had made his judgment a long time ago.) I stood still, stupidly waiting. I knew it would be over soon. Another terse remark, deadpanned in that unplaceable accent, an innuendo, a verbal lure, and I would cut him dead, or worse. But I was wrong.

"Ever read Chopenauer?" Barney asked, whispering again.

The question confused me. I looked for a trick. Barney did that to you. You were always prepared for a secret side. "No," I said. I could see Barney shaking his head in the dark, as though I was hopeless. And damned if I didn't feel inadequate in the face of his disapproval.

"Too heavy for you?" he asked.

"I wouldn't say that."

Barney looked to the right and the left, massaging himself to keep warm.

"Do you know what Chopenauer said about women?" he then asked.

"Yes."

"How do you know?"

"You told us. Back in the States."

"What did I tell you?"

"Women get pregnant. It's what they were made for."

"What they were made for," he said, sounding disgusted. "It's always so simple for you Americans. You're just like children. No subtleness. Maybe you should read something else besides Dick Tracy."

That stung. I wanted to say that I didn't read Dick Tracy anymore. I finished with that long ago. But I had read Thucydides, Plato, and Aristotle, and I probably could get interested in Schopenhauer, too. But it was too late to say all that. I could feel Barney withdrawing. The cryptic exchange was over. He wasn't interested in the likes of me. I had made a wrong assumption. I had been prepared for an unwelcome confrontation—he had prepared me for it—and all there was in the end was verbal dithering.

After another moment or two of silence, Barney turned his back and resumed his walk. We were once again merely two guards, on nighttime duty in a Normandy orchard, who were not supposed to talk to each other. The hours passed. The bright constellations seemed to move with the moon, and our shift soon ended.

I don't think Barney Barnato gave me a thought after that. I wasn't interesting enough for him. I lacked intellectual clout; I didn't care sufficiently about his mysteries. Later, I learned that there were others in the third platoon who had suffered the same attention—and in embarrassed silence, too. It seemed that none of us considered it an honor.

AFTER weeks of inactivity, Paul Willis began to steal again. As old victims, Bern and I laughed about it sardonically, even though we weren't quite sure where the joke was. Willis had again become the old opaque Willis we had known in Tennessee and South Carolina, unreadable and ungiving, feckless and weird. Gone were his adult concerns about the squad's future, about Fedderman's place in it, and our urgent need for harmony and mutual support, as he had expressed it aboard the SS *Argentina* and later acted on. What Bern and I felt, instead, was a sudden shakiness that we soon began to share, an insecurity that undermined the active surface of our lives— beneath the forced marches and the bayonet drills and all the other exhausting routines—and the beginnings of a familiar, wormy fear about what lay ahead.

Nobody wanted to talk about being scared. Our pride and self-esteem were involved, indeed threatened, and, beyond that, we had no useful vocabulary to describe such a state. How do you talk about fear when fear is fast becoming the chief currency of life? Willis's behavior, as strange to us as ever, became our barometer of possible disaster, and we began to read him daily for sinister omens.

Soon after that, Rocky disappeared one night, slipping out casually after dark through a hedgerow and staying away for forty-eight hours. While he was gone, we handled everything ourselves, much like a commune, with Barney, as the oldest among us, taking over as acting squad leader and Arch sticking his nose in every now and then to check things out and bolster our morale. We did all right.

When Rocky came back, he was clean-shaven, his hair freshly cut, eyes clear. Nothing was ever asked of him about his adventure (to my knowledge), and nothing was ever explained. He just picked up where he had left us. It was a typical Rocky performance, done with a deft and smooth touch, but like Willis's thefts, it too somehow seemed to carry a warning. A kind of social deviance was suddenly in the air.

Bern caught me alone one day after the midday meal. "I think I'll go to Mass on Sunday," he said, as though I had asked him. The Catholics in C Company held weekly Mass out in the open, in an adjoining orchard, using an improvised altar. It was always well attended. But Bern and I rarely talked about religion. It was a minefield.

"I haven't been to Mass since we landed in Cherbourg," he went on, with a defensive growl.

"Well, sir, if that's what you want." I was eyeing him skeptically, but I didn't mean to sound sarcastic. I knew better than that, in the face of religious convictions. But what had happened to his doubts, which he had expressed to me just once in a muted conversation that was over almost before it had begun?

"That's what I want," he said.

"Good."

Arch blew a whistle to get us back into the field. "So you've returned to God," I said.

"If I ever left." Defiant Bern.

"Right."

I guess there was nothing else to say. It was Bern's conversation, still muted. He had launched it like a shell from a strange artillery piece, and it had landed right on target, but why, I asked myself, were we suddenly having this exchange, at that particular moment?

RUMORS of the day, wildly flapping across the Normandy landscape like broken-winged ravens:

. . . the Germans had asked for a cease-fire, unconditionally.

. . . fifteen hundred American POWs had been massacred in a German POW camp east of Munich—in another version, outside Nuremberg.

. . . the Russians had surrendered. Stalin was dead, by his own hand.

. . . the YD has been chosen as the American division to share in the administration of Paris with the French and British, post-liberation.

. . . two hundred Japanese suicide bombers had flattened Seattle by sneaking in over the North Pole and dropping themselves and their explosives on the city.

. . . we would get our typhus booster shots within three days.

. . . Marlene Dietrich was coming our way with the USO, accompanied by her pal, Papa Hemingway.

. . . Eisenhower and Montgomery had engaged in an open fistfight in front of Allied troops over the disastrous airborne landings in Holland.

. . . ditto Michael Antonovich and Francis J. Gallagher, over other matters.


WE KNEW how the last rumor got started. For the first time, Antonovich and Gallagher had disagreed in public. It was over the use of the word "relevant," or seemed to be, and it took place in front of the whole company right after reveille one morning.

"It's just not revelant!" Antonovich shouted at Gallagher as we were breaking ranks. That stopped some of us in our tracks. Our captain and lieutenant never shouted at each other in front of the troops. We waited to see what would happen. In a moment, Gallagher bent down, pretended to pick up a cigarette butt, pretended to strip it, then straightened up. All very slowly. Still, we hung around. Something compelled us. Gallagher waited a few more seconds before answering, as though he was considering several alternatives.

"The word is 'relevant,'" he finally said, very cool and loud.

"That's what I said," Antonovich snapped.

"No, it wasn't," Gallagher answered, beginning to walk away. "But the hell with it."

Antonovich reached out as though to stop Gallagher from heading off, but seemed to think better of it. "What are you two staring at?" he yelled at Bern and Fedderman, who were still standing there gaping. "Move your butts."

And what was that all about, we asked each other later, officers behaving so pettily in front of their men. I never learned, although I suspected, unhappily, that it had come from deep out of the shared past. All I knew was that the exchange—minimal as it was, bare-boned as well as sharp—unsettled the company. Nobody was happy to have witnessed it. There was an unspoken feeling among us that if it had happened that morning out in the open, without camouflage, then it had happened before in private and would happen again.

And it didn't help much to believe that my man had won. Or to suspect that he probably always did.

AT THE end of the week, we got our typhus boosters, painful ones, too, and a day later they—somebody— ordered short-arm inspection for the entire division. This meant fourteen thousand Yankee penises—give or take— on limp display, not all at one time, of course. We hadn't had a short-arm since we left the States. There was no need for one. No one had even spoken to a French woman, much less touched one. Unless Rocky Hubbell had during his forty-eight-hour caper, which seemed likely. But the rest of us were locked inside our hedgerows, strictly monitored, and, in any case, every brothel in Normandy was off-limits.

Everybody hated short-arm. It was insidious, a brilliant technique for invading our tentative sense of self and privacy. Penis, anus, testicles; cocks, assholes, balls. Nothing was sacred. When the order went out for short-arm, a mortified groan went up from the YD. And you couldn't get out of it by volunteering for KP or latrine duty. Everyone was subject.

Our time came. We lined up. Behind the first squad stood the second squad, joyous as always at the idea of watching us being humiliated. They jeered under their breath, talked dirty, laughed at us, as though they weren't going to have to go through the same process themselves as soon as we were finished. Behind the second squad was the third, just as scabrous, hating the second squad perhaps more than the second squad hated us. While this was going on, two doctors, whom we had never seen before, wearing the caduceus on their jacket lapels, gave us the eye as they chatted briefly with Arch and Antonovich and Gallagher, doing the amenities before going to work.

In another moment, we dropped our pants and undershorts at a command from Gallagher. (Actually, Willis dropped Bern's undershorts, which he happened to be wearing at the moment.)

We stood there exposed as the doctors proceeded along the line from man to man, delicately using their middle fingers to feel behind each scrotum at the point where it joined the pelvis.

"Cough." Rocky coughed, blushing furiously, I saw.

"Look to the right." Johnson did as he was told.

"Cough." Brewster managed a dry hack.

"Pull back the foreskin, please." Willis responded eagerly.

"Do you wash there regularly?"

Willis nodded.

"It's especially important to wash there, son. You know about smegma, don't you?" A faint distaste suddenly became evident, as the doctor asked his question.

"Now cough." Willis coughed.

"Again."

And so on, down the line of the first squad, through Natale, Keaton, me, and on to Fedderman, who, as in most things, was last again.

"Cough." Fedderman had trouble producing a fake cough for the doctors. He had to try twice.

The doctors took a moment then to consult together. I could hear their soft, professional voices whispering away. What had they seen? What had they felt as they fingered our testicles? More whispering. A clearing of throats. Then, apparently satisfied, they turned to walk behind us, in front of the second squad, which was still enjoying itself for the moment, jeering under its breath, still talking dirty. "Oh, *là*," someone said, trying to sound lascivious. What a bunch.

"Quiet, back there," Gallagher ordered.

Then we heard the command we'd been waiting for. "Bend over," one of the docs said. And the second order: "Spread your cheeks and make it snappy, fellows." Somehow, Army doctors never managed to sound like real officers.

They passed down the line behind us, looking up Johnson's spread cheeks, up Rocky Hubbell's dusty Texas gully, up Paul Willis's, Brewster's, Natale's, up mine, then up Bern Keaton's verdant Irish dale, and finally . . . what was this? What did we hear? Ira Fedderman was refusing to reveal himself, refusing to bend over and spread his buttocks for the benefit of two strangers. Could it be true? My God! Somebody hooted in the second squad at this protest. There was nervous laughter all around us. The doctors repeated the order, then Gallagher rushed over and thrust his forefinger into Fedderman's pigeon chest and shouted something. The two doctors looked bemused. Fedderman stood very still, chin up, at attention.

"Do what you're told, for Chrissake!" Rocky yelled from down the line, his fatigue pants saucered around his ankles. It was getting chilly, standing out in the morning air like this. What was going to happen?

Fedderman held firm. I could almost feel his sphincter tighten. (God bless him.) I think we all felt it. Antonovich was now into the act, looking walleyed. Always subject to extremes, he threatened a court-martial. At the threat, Gallagher looked disgusted. A house divided. Gallagher shrugged apologetically at the doctors. One of them smiled back. He was amused. Genuinely so. Had he ever seen this kind of resistance before?

Fedderman still stood at attention, his shirttails barely covering his powerful behind. His fat thighs were pressed tightly together, his swampy genitals open to the entire Norman countryside. This went on for another few minutes, until the doctors decided to move on to the second squad. They were finally embarrassed, along with almost everyone else; they couldn't wait to get away from us. Antonovich and Gallagher, assisted by Rocky and Arch, who had just arrived on the scene, hauled Fedderman off, marching him between them, like a convict, to company headquarters. First they let him pull up his pants. We watched them go, admiring Ira Fedderman, who was thin-lipped and scared-looking. In that moment, I almost loved him. At one corner of his mouth, as he marched away, hung a saliva bubble of anxiety, ready to burst.

They barely had a chance to get Fedderman's wind up. It was over almost as soon as it began. The fact was that our orders had arrived at last. The ones we had been waiting for for weeks. But they weren't for General Simpson's Ninth Army. They were for the Third Army, Patton's Army, which was a world away in Alsace-Lorraine. (It was goodbye to "Roses of Picardy.") At the news, which was spread by Antonovich in a voice pinched by excitement, I could begin to smell the fear (my own first) as we began to feverishly pack for the trip across France to Alsace. "Al-sotz," Antonovich called it while Gallagher made a condescending face behind him. We were on our way by truck within hours, whipped along by Arch's noisy fervor. What a racket again, what a roar, worse than Cherbourg. Fedderman's overworked sphincter—everybody's sphincter, for that matter—was probably tighter than ever as we left our apple orchard. I knew mine was, and it was destined to stay tight for a long time to come.

# FIVE

## *Île-de-France*

BY LATE afternoon, we were approaching Paris. That was the good word, passed along during breaks from one truck to another via our drivers, who were becoming the bearers of all rumors. At the news, my absurd hopes rose. Maybe we would have a day or two in the city. Maybe I would get to see Paris at last, however briefly. Maybe . . . But I knew better. Certain kinds of rumors could never be believed, mainly those that promised pleasure. And Paris had not figured in Captain Antonovich's hastily compressed review of our future, which he delivered to us breathlessly just before we left Normandy. Lunéville was where we were headed. Pronounced "Looney-ville" by Antonovich, again with Gallagher frowning condescendingly behind him. There had not been a word about Paris.

Antonovich had told us that Lunéville was in "Al-sotz," somewhere in the mysterious east. There we would relieve the Fourth Armored Division. The division, spearhead of Patton's Third Army, was anchored just beyond the city of

Nancy, in the slow-rising hills that eventually ran up to the Vosges Mountains near the German border. The men of the Fourth Armored were heroes to half the world. They had led the race across France after the Normandy break-out and would have crossed into Germany itself if they had not run out of fuel and ammunition. The mere sound of their name intimidated me and everyone else. While we replaced the Fourth on what had become a static front, the division would pull out for rest and reconditioning in the area behind the Third Army lines. It was simple enough. And Paris was nowhere in the calculation.

I actually thought I saw the city for a moment glimmering straight ahead of our convoy, miles in front of us, a vast circular stone mirage set in its river basin, white as the moon. So it seemed to me as the sight of it brought me to my feet in our truck. Those soft urban hills molding the horizon, that dull iron tower rigidly thrusting upward on the banks of the river, the silver river itself gently moving west on our left. It was really Paris. Everybody then stood up to catch a glimpse, falling over themselves. The trucks swayed around a curve, the city came closer, a weak cheer went up.

"We're all going to get laid!" Willis shouted. "French-style."

Everybody laughed at this prediction, wistfully, and of course with an edge. In the next minute, the convoy suddenly veered south, rumbling over rustic cobblestones for a couple of miles or so before turning east again, while to the north the elusive white city began to disappear in the late afternoon mist, and we were left with only road signs for consolation. Versailles, Rambouillet, Chartres, St.-Germain, they read, on their neat little military markers; Sceaux, Vaux-le-Vicomte, Fontainebleau —dozens of arrows, it seemed, crazily pointing in every direction.

There was no question about it, we were heading straight for Lunéville, where the war was waiting for us.

Conversation stopped then; suddenly nobody had the heart for it. Silence set in—the soldiers' deeply depressed, introverted silence, marked by a kind of low-grade fever that affected everybody. We were even trying to move physically apart from each other—politely, you might say, without giving offense, as a way of protecting ourselves. It was strange, this sudden defensive impulse, the need to withdraw, shared by all. Bern didn't speak to me, I didn't speak to him. Fedderman shunned us both, locked into his own one-man universe. We didn't even look at each other. The rest of the squad acted the same way. All this on behalf of our sanity, collective and individual; all this surfacing from our most profound instincts and fears, long before we had reached the flash-point of actual danger.

We drove on into a calm twilight, past quiet villages and empty town squares. We were sore from the wooden seats we slouched on, and hungry again. Everyone needed sleep. Ten miles passed, fifteen. Finally, after another half-hour of quick stopping and starting (the jolting kind that wrenches the bowels), as the long convoy line tried to put itself in order, we pulled up alongside a vast plain that seemed to be the size of several football fields. We stared at it, impressed. Motors quieted, there was another silence as we sat there waiting. Woods lined the field on both sides of the road, artful Gallic scenery that looked planned and well-regulated, all of it park-like. This was no green American-style wilderness, no informal place to improvise Tarzan or cowboy-and-Indian games. Someone took care of this, someone cultivated it every day. Someone was responsible.

"Fontainebleau," the word went out as we de-trucked, moaning with relief as our stiff joints found the earth again. (Fontainebleau, I thought dimly. The name had a vague resonance that I couldn't quite place. Louis XIV? Napoleon? Josephine? I wasn't sure.) There was the usual fifteen minutes of milling around as we gathered our equipment, a quick, nervous examination of our imposing new surroundings, and then, at a command that must have come from Gangplank Paul himself, wherever he was, the entire 26th infantry division moved out onto the plain and, in near total silence, pitched tents in straight, orderly lines, forming an immense gridiron, one company after another, down the entire length of the open space. There was hardly a sound, just the clank of shovels against stone and rifle butts hammering wooden poles for our tents into the hard, resisting soil. We barely said a word as we worked. Nobody complained. The setting seemed to call for that.

Then the cooks built their fires, dozens of them, washing up began, and soon we were eating our evening meal as the sun began to disappear. There was the sound of mess gear being readied and the homey smell of coffee everywhere. When total darkness finally came down, thousands of cigarettes lighted the night air like armies of fireflies, a hum of subdued conversation spread from one end of the division to the other as we visited each other, and in another hour or so we began to drift off, in the huge encampment, to our own tents, looking for sleep.

But first our orders: Do not make a mess. Strip all cigarettes. Bury all waste. Leave this place in the morning as you found it today. This is Fontainebleau. Thus spake Rene Archambault.

As though we understood. As though, if we understood, we would care. But again we did as we were told. Except for Rocky's brief excursion and mine, as well as Fedderman's perverse little short-arm rebellion, which had secretly thrilled us all and made him notorious in the entire regiment, when didn't we?

This is Fontainebleau, Rene Archambault repeated. "Fountainblue. Ecch," Fedderman said, shaking his head in mock-disgust at Arch's pronunciation.

In another half-hour, we were asleep. Our drivers, members of a black regiment, slept apart from us, behind their trucks on the other side of the road. This segregation bothered me. It bothered Bern and Fedderman, too. It made us self-conscious, they from New Jersey and New York and me from Baltimore, Maryland. We looked at each other guiltily, exchanged a few sharp words on the subject, smiled sharp, knowing smiles, and turned our backs. But the contradictions and the guilt stayed with us, even as we could hear shouts of laughter and heavy cursing continue into the night from across the road.

"Mu-tha!"

"Fuck-a!"

How we loved that. We couldn't get enough of it. Mu-tha! Fuck-a! I wanted to be able to talk like that. We all did. The smart kids. Fat chance.


SLEEP was fitful that night. Fedderman's asthmatic rasps marked the hours, bringing me nervously awake every time they reached a new climax. When they did, I went outside to pee, where there was always somebody else doing the same. Sharing a pup tent was still problematic for me. It was the old story: my obsessions. There were noises and there were smells, but mostly there were smells. Fedderman's odor was as unique as a fingerprint, a curious mixture of sweat, oil, and, as I remember, something like burned rubber that seemed to emerge from the very core of his body. It could be overwhelming. Also, Fedderman's equipment, as always, was thrown everywhere. But so was mine that night. Combat boots, ammo belts, rifles, all mixed together in sloppy piles; there would be no morning inspection by Rocky at Fontainebleau. I awoke feeling edgy and unprepared, a cloud of vague anxiety trailing me as it had since we left Normandy. I crept out of the tent on my hands and knees, trying not to wake Fedderman. He clicked his teeth in his sleep as I went.

It was not quite six. Smoke from our cooking fires already clouded the early morning air; wood burned with its delicious smell. Here and there, along the road, I could see drivers checking out their trucks, part by part, exactly as we checked out our weapons. In one of the tent-lines, somebody from B Company was shaving out of his helmet, a hand-mirror propped in front of him. A couple of tents down, in our own line, Willis was on his feet stretching. I could almost hear him purr. Alongside him, Barney Barnato was brushing his teeth. Stray figures wandered about, looking for latrines. Everyone else was still asleep. There was another half-hour to reveille. I liked the early morning hour before reveille, its clarity, its stillness and sense of solitude. I always had.

Standing there in that near-perfect light, I began to think about home. A terrible idea, as always. Thinking about home was a self-made trap that I had to avoid. At home, I had discovered on my only furlough that the old familiar grammar of life had become unreadable. They spoke another language there, about things that no longer mattered, using a vocabulary out of another time. Thinking about it would demoralize me. I had been through that before. I tried some calisthenics as a distraction, jumping stuff, clumsy push-ups. Physical activity sometimes helped. After that I brushed my teeth hard, until it hurt, drawing blood and spitting it out on the treasured Fontainebleau soil. Did it make me feel better? I don't know, nor did it matter, because suddenly there was a disruption that wiped out all nostalgia for the moment.

I heard the sound of hoofbeats nearby, a strange, plodding reverberation that seemed to come from inside the earth itself. I looked up. Willis was pointing toward the road, grinning his sly grin and shaking his head from side to side, as though to say, You guys'll never believe this.

When I turned, I saw two riders come into view, both of them young girls, barely pubescent, I guessed, cantering along at a deliberate, modest pace. They were looking neither right nor left, not at us nor at our drivers, who were already having their breakfast alongside their trucks. On and on the girls rode, not at all fast, unconscious of us, or seeming to be. I remember asking myself, as I watched them, How could they pretend not to be aware of us?

Their hair, hanging loose down their backs, was held at their necks by black ribbons, which struck me as a strange funereal accent. They wore jodhpurs, gleaming riding-boots, and long-sleeved white blouses that shimmered in the early sun; and they were posting, I thought, in a slightly exaggerated way (not that I am an expert), rising a little too high in the saddle, pausing a split second, then falling again, slowly. Showing off, I guessed. They were very good at it, very controlled, and kept an exact pace with each other, in the authoritative way of trained riders who know their business. I had to admire them. They looked wonderful. When I glanced at Willis a moment later, he was still grinning.

Then a third rider came into view, a young boy this time, younger than the two girls, following their trail by about fifty feet. Maybe he was ten or eleven. By now, Fedderman and Bern were at my side, Fedderman wearing only his underwear. Perhaps a couple of hundred others were also watching as the three riders, the boy looking as though he was in excruciating pain (you could tell how helpless he felt being part of this trio, how mortified he was to be trailing the two girls), trotted alongside our trucks for another moment or two, and then, with a sudden shout from the girls, rode off at high speed. You could still hear their hoofbeats after they disappeared into the woods.

This is Fontainebleau, I told myself in the ghostly silence that followed. This is the Île-de-France, the very heart of France, heart of its aristocratic heart. Yes. But I hardly knew what I meant by that.

"Holy shit," Willis said, still shaking his head.

"Cunts." This from Barney Barnato.

Bern made a face. Certain words profoundly offended him.

"Noblesse oblige," Fedderman said, beginning one of his lectures. "French variety," he added. Then, after turning back to our tent: "They probably own the joint. All of it.

Upper upper. And all that." He spoke with a fake Brit accent, to make sure we got all the implications of what he was saying.

A creaky bugle began to blow reveille. This broke the spell. We made a rush for our mess gear. A huge clamor rose in the morning sky, the noise of fourteen thousand men suddenly resurrected from sleep. We were getting ready for another move. In our rush, Arch reminded us, we would not make a litter. We would be especially careful today. We would leave this place exactly as we found it: perfect.

But I was still thinking about what Fedderman had said. I knew he was right. Fedderman was smart about things like that. What he didn't know he figured out, and unlike many smart people, he almost always came to the right conclusions. No brilliant fool, he. Noblesse oblige, he had said. French variety. I was sure those girls owned the joint, that we were camped—by very special permission—on their family's ancient estate grounds. (And their suffering little brother? their slave? their young protector? What about him?) Maybe they deserved their little joke, I decided, to pretend that we didn't exist, that we were invisible, while their own lives continued on a normal course, under normal assumptions, in their own front yard. It was a sure way to remind us of who we really were, in a style we wouldn't forget.

But it was a nasty business, to my mind.

THERE was a brisk trade in books before we left. Most of the readers in the battalion knew each other by now, and we ran along the adjoining tent-lines calling out titles, as though we were street peddlers. I got Eric Ambler's *Journey Into Fear* (a title in which I read no ironies) for Michael Innes's *Hamlet, Revenge!*—the heavy scent of Levantine musk for the clear taste of high tea, a fair exchange in my view. Bern brought away *Tortilla Flat,* heavily dog-eared, and Fedderman traded Will James's *Cowboy* for *The Late George Apley,* feeling that it was time "to finally take a sounding," in his words, of John P. Marquand, whom he had never read. Even Brewster, I discovered, was at it; that was good news about Brewster, I thought. This business of swapping books was very satisfying. We felt that we got true value and more. I had also been offered A. J. Cronin's *The Citadel,* Howard Spring's *My Son, My Son,* and James Hilton's *Lost Horizon,* and rejected all three—for snob reasons, probably, because they were too popular. Fedderman, I'm sorry to say, shared that attitude.

But none of us would be without something to read. We were stocked for the future, books packed into each fatigue pocket. A book marked the shortest, straightest, and most invigorating lifeline to the real world—the world outside that would continue on its way, in its own orbit, no matter what might happen to us. That's what I believed. That's what most of the readers in the Yankee Division believed.

WE BOARDED the trucks, cracking gallows jokes with the drivers, who laughed at everything we said. They knew that as soon as they dumped us in Al-sotz they would be able to turn around and instantly head back for Normandy, leaving us deserted. We tried to settle back on our hard wooden benches, our buttocks becoming slatted as we faced each other in the truck in two straight lines. Our equipment was piled between us in a mound of canvas, metal, and K and C rations. Paul Willis, too, had spread himself out between us on the floor of the truck, amid the junk, as though he was going on a hayride, while Rocky, who made no objections to the mess, sat at the open end like the perfect squad leader, his foot hoisted up onto a metal brace, scribbling intently in a tiny pad he always carried with him. Each truck began to rev up along the endless jittery line of machines, making a swelling gravelly noise that choked all conversation; all this and more—shouting officers, resentful NCOs, blasé GIs—combined, almost simultaneously, into a single human and mechanical roar. Thus the division began to move east and north again, past the great Fontainebleau plain that we had camped on for the night, now stripped of all Yankee Division litter, latrine holes filled in, fires out, ashes damped and spread—if not pristine, then damn near—almost the way we had found it the day before, almost. Then I caught Bern Keaton staring blankly at me from the other side of the truck. He seemed wholly abstracted by reverie and what I read as a kind of silent dread that we all knew. As I stared back, Fedderman, alongside me, always alongside me, began to snore lightly in his second sleep of the morning. I couldn't help myself then. I was again smothered by the cataclysmic idea of home—the agonized figures of mother, father, and sister saying good-bye on our front porch, the pink blooms of our rose garden, the aging blue Chevy (a fading piece of used metal from the late thirties), our talismanic Chickering piano, standing in a corner of the immaculate living room, with my music resting on it—

Beethoven, Chopin, Czerny. Home had not yet finished with me. It was always there, as inevitable as gravity. I was trapped, along with my buddies, and familiar clusters of hives began to form on the back of my neck.


THE TRUCKS rolled on, the morning lightened. I began to hum a little tune to myself—something or other by Irving Berlin, I think—on which I fastened obsessively. I was deliberately trying to lull myself into a kind of oblivion that I hoped would last for the next couple of hours, for the rest of the morning and afternoon, with any luck, trying to quiet my rising blood while I stared over Bern's shoulder at the passing scene—towns, squares, road signs, churches, farms, an occasional Frenchman staring blankly back at me from the side of the road without acknowledging that I was there. I could never tell what the French thought of us.

And still we didn't talk.

Rheims, the road signs read.

Verdun.

Hours later, Nancy, Sarrebourg, Lunéville.

"Looney-ville," as everyone now called it. And Looney-ville it would remain, even though we never got to see it, never even came close.

# SIX

# *Holes*

THIS GUY kept smiling at me—this stranger, actually. He'd been smiling at Johnson and me for fifteen minutes. He couldn't stop. I could tell that he was helpless. He told us his name was Smith or Smitt or Schmidt, something like that. I couldn't make it out and Johnson was no help. It was hard to concentrate on what Smith was saying at two o'clock in the morning, in the pitch black of the Alsatian countryside. Every sense seemed to be diminished by the darkness: sight, hearing, touch, even taste; only smell remained intact, in the face of an acrid assault by a concatenation of cordite, cigarette smoke, stale urine, excrement, earth, human sweat, and the chemical excess of our own pungent fear, which, like a dog, I could sniff out and clearly identify. What a stink! Johnson's was as powerful as mine, with a palpable mountain presence of its own. Nobody in the first squad failed the fear test.

Putting Johnson and me together was Rocky's idea. By then we knew that he liked to shift us around, mixing it up: Bern and me, Fedderman and Johnson, Fedderman and me, Johnson and me. (He kept Brewster and Natale together for unexplained reasons of his own; perhaps it was only because they were still new to the unit.) It was supposed to keep us fresh and alert, to help us face change and rethink our responsibilities, and to learn to be resilient. It was supposed to keep us interested, too. Maybe it did. It certainly forced us to think about each other.

Fedderman now belonged to Bern. They shared a hole together maybe fifteen, twenty feet away, the hole sited so that between us we could offer up a neat little crossfire in case of an enemy attack. That is, if we were on the mark. This new arrangement confirmed me as first assistant BAR man. If Johnson was wounded or killed, I was it. That meant two lives I had to pray for now. I tried not to think about it too much; there was a lot I was trying to push away that night when we arrived at the front. Anyway, I never prayed; I only made deals with myself—the usual promises of good behavior if I survived.

This guy, this stranger, told us that enemy attacks were rare, but nighttime probes, on a small scale, were common. He warned us that we had better keep our eyes open, especially after dark. After dark was the sensitive time. He could hardly get the words out fast enough; it was almost a babble. Then he smiled some more, while we took it all in. Could we believe him? Was his advice reliable? Or were enthusiasm and a sense of relief carrying him away? His buddy, with whom he had shared this hole, had already pulled out for the rear, while he remained behind to brief us. They had probably tossed a coin for the honor and he had lost. I thought he was doing an okay job, except for all the smiling. I could have done without that; it put an edge on every word.

Briefings were going on all along the line in holes just like ours as the Yankee Division slipped nervously into the positions the Fourth Armored Division was leaving with such open joy. They had done a careful job when they dug in, as though they were preparing for a long stay. The holes were deep and self-contained, meant for living and protection; ours had a neat ledge cut into one wall for supplies. The hole itself was shaped like a trapezoid, and there was plenty of room for two men. At the moment, it held three comfortably. I didn't know whether the trapezoid shape had a purpose or not, and I forgot to ask.

It had rained nearly all the way to Nancy once we were out of the Île-de-France, but the rain had stopped now. After unloading from the trucks in the dark, a couple of miles to the rear, Johnson took a bad spill in the fresh mud on our way on foot up to the front—no real damage done, just muck and wet filth covering him everywhere. An annoyance; another thorn. There was a smell stuck to him, too, that was unidentifiable; probably cow dung, I thought.

Johnson was beginning to show nerves for the first time since I had known him, snorting like a horse as we squatted there in the hole, listening to Smith, or Smitt, or Schmidt talk on. While he talked, I watched a huge moon drift to the west. Scudding clouds veiled it like handmaidens. Beyond Smith's words, there was a lunar stillness everywhere, except for the strange horsey sounds Johnson was making. I began to count the stars, listening to Smith with one ear, to distract myself—a hopeless job. Smith was still smiling. He was jubilant to be leaving for the rear.

The more jubilant he seemed, the more nervous we became. And he knew it.

"So," he said, suddenly holding out his right hand, as though we had just struck a deal. "Can't think of anything else."

We shook hands, first Johnson, then me. "Good luck," he said. Then he was gone, rifle slung over his shoulder, heading to the rear in a slouching run. We would all soon become expert at running in that slouch. Down the line, I could hear Fedderman's voice. He was in one of his states, as we all were. Oh, God, that whine . . . Bern was telling him to shut up, sounding irritable. In another moment, Rocky was at our hole.

"You guys all right?"

Johnson snorted. I said nothing.

"Speak up," Rocky said, down on one knee so he could whisper to us. In the moonlight, his bony Texan face looked anxious; all his features were creased together.

"You're going to get knocked off like that," I said, meaning the silhouette he made kneeling there.

He crouched lower and hurriedly pointed out his own foxhole, which he told us he shared with Willis and Barnato. Brewster and Natale were on the right somewhere, he said, pointing again, along with Bern and Fedderman. That accounted for everyone in the first squad. In the dark, Rocky then traced the position of the rest of the platoon. The best I could tell from what he said was that together we made a jagged line, a zigzag, with intervals of fifteen to twenty feet between each foxhole. Maybe they were even closer. Taken together, Rocky explained in a rush, the foxholes made a position; and the position was

built to a plan that he didn't bother to explain. Maybe he
didn't know the plan himself. That would be the way
things usually worked with us. Then Rocky left.

I thought I could make out a few hills up ahead, two or
three hundred yards in front of us. Maybe "hills" is too
strong a word; "rises" is probably more accurate. A few
rises then, nothing dramatic, overlooking our own position. Given a choice, of course, I would have preferred to
look down at them, rather than up. But it was hard to figure out in the dark, so I let it go; I would worry about it in
the morning when everything would be revealed. I
checked my watch, to have something to do. Three
o'clock. The moon was still bright.

"You all right?" I asked Johnson.

He was lining up some grenades on the ledge, alongside
boxes of K rations, placing them in a neat row. Johnson was
always very neat. It was how he did everything. I guessed
he was okay even though he was still snorting while he
worked. Then, far away on our left, a red flare rose slowly
in the night sky, arched, sputtered, and hung in the air for
a second or two before falling. A real bloom, in the middle
of the night. Johnson and I both watched it, the strange
light diffusing brightly against the moving clouds. I could
see Bern and Fedderman watching, too, and Willis and
Barnato—we were all heads up in our foxholes, pale Yankee
faces lightly pinked by the red glare hanging above us. The
whole division was probably watching.

Ours or theirs? I wondered, meaning the flare. Where
were they exactly? Meaning the Germans.

And where were we?

Rocky, like our helpful pal from the Fourth Armored,
had forgotten to tell us. Maybe Rocky didn't know. Maybe

he hadn't been filled in yet. But I wanted to know. It seemed urgent. Where we were and where they were.

"Face front," was Johnson's advice when I asked him, "and you'll sure as hell see them sooner or later." For Johnson, that was a mouthful, and it served. I stopped worrying about it.

THE following night, Johnson and I were chosen for outpost duty.

We had spent the day quietly acclimating ourselves and trying to catch up on sleep. Everything was quiet as we all settled in—a lucky break for us. Maybe, after all, we had relieved the Fourth without the Germans learning about it. That would mark a real achievement.

Meanwhile, Johnson, always fastidious, had placed his shaving equipment on the ledge in our hole, alongside his grenades and boxes of K rations, leaving an equal amount of space for me. To the inch, exactly; I watched him measure it. I liked that, after the mess I had lived with and grown used to with Ira Fedderman. I had a pretty good idea what Fedderman's foxhole looked like this morning. I glanced over our parapet—the Fourth had really constructed their defenses—but could see nothing, neither Bern nor Fedderman. Yet there was a sense of activity out there, a settling-in everywhere down the line. Metallic noises, the sound of a shovel somewhere, mutterings, whispers. Even, briefly, the hollow echo of artillery fire to the east that made everything seem real for the moment.

In the morning light, the rises I had seen the night before now appeared as dun-colored ridges, not steep, not long, but humped in camel-like folds here and there, as though they were hiding something. Undoubtedly they were. But they didn't look forbidding or menacing. They looked innocent. It was raining again, a light drizzle that created a floating mist all around us. This gave me an illusion of protection and invisibility, as rain often did. If I couldn't see the Germans, my theory went, they couldn't see me.

Rocky checked us out every couple of hours. We knew that he was trying to keep busy in a responsible way, making sure that we felt his presence and authority as the perfect squad leader. At first, that morning, Rocky crawled from hole to hole on his knees and elbows, carbine cradled in his arms, just as the books said. Later, probably feeling safer when the day wore on without incident, he rose to a crouch as he made his connections among us. (He was accompanied once or twice, as I remember, by Arch, who seemed to appear out of nowhere, asking a lot of edgy questions; Arch's questions were always edgy, wherever we were.) Everything was still calm, still quiet. Wet, too. We might have been on bivouac at Camp Jackson or maneuvering in the Tennessee foothills in the spring rains. By mid-afternoon of the first day, I began to feel a little giddy. It was a touch of overconfidence, accompanied perhaps by a rise in blood pressure. Excitement, I knew, could do that to me. I had survived, without a serious scare, for sixteen hours. We were on the line, in position, and we were intact.

At four o'clock, Rocky arrived for the third visit of the day. Flat on his belly this time and without looking at us, he told Johnson and me that we were to go on outpost duty from midnight until dawn—or rather, the moment before dawn, the few seconds just before the first light rises. (He found several ways of saying this, to emphasize how important it was.) He told us that on outpost we were to be alert to all strange sounds, all movement, to anything that felt like a threat. Our real job was to warn C Company of any impending dawn attack that would most likely come from those folded hills that rose in front of us. (I eyed them as Rocky talked on, trying to remember their outlines and imagine the Germans hidden inside them.) We were to sit in the outpost trench face-to-face, feet touching. The pressure of our feet against each other, which we would regulate as needed, would make sure that we stayed awake. He paused at this before going on, so that we would remember it. One of us, he then added, would face in the direction of the enemy lines, the other would face ours. That seemed obvious. At three o'clock, approximately the midway point, we would change positions.

"Any questions?" He waited a moment. "You better get some sleep," he said then, appearing reluctant to leave us. "You got all that now?" he asked.

Poor bastard. I could tell how worried he was. It was like looking into a mirror and seeing myself. I suppose he was feeling guilty, too.

"And where the hell is the outpost?" I finally asked. I was already shaking a little, my usual way.

"What an asshole," Rocky said, meaning himself. (We always seemed to be forgetting to exchange essential information in the first squad.) He pointed straight ahead. "That's it out there," he said. "Maybe a hundred yards, a little to the left of that pile of shit. See it?"

Yes, I saw it.

.   .   .

DUSK came soon enough. Johnson and I began to open some of my C rations. I preferred C to K rations; they really filled you up, even had a taste, but you had to try to forget that they looked like dog food. I could tell that Johnson was as abstracted as I was, that he was beginning to lose his focus little by little. He spat a lot of thick, phlegmy stuff, and chewed on some hangnails, but the snorting had stopped. I was even worse, almost out of control, and trying desperately to hide it. I couldn't even open my can of C rations properly. It was a simple, familiar task, repeated a thousand times during my infantry training, yet I sliced my thumb open, deep in the fleshy part, with the jagged edge of the half-open can, cursing myself when I saw the blood. It was a piece of childish clumsiness worthy of Ira Fedderman. It took me half a minute to get my self-possession back, to try to smile as I felt my thumb begin to throb.

"You're really bleeding," Johnson said.

"It's nothing." I spoke with all the piety of the professional stoic. "Where's the first-aid stuff?"

We spent five minutes trying to stop the bleeding, and finally, bandaged and abashed, I was able to settle back against the wall of the foxhole and slowly eat my rations, in control of myself at last. Johnson, too, was better after this tiny crisis. He stopped spitting and the noises he had made did not come back. We had four hours to midnight.

"You all right?" I asked.

Johnson nodded.

That was how we passed the time, asking each other obvious questions, checking our watches, synchronizing them, napping, defecating into our helmets (twice each) and dumping it onto the ground behind us—and slowly, as it grew darker, hour by hour, losing ourselves to the thought of the lonely job ahead.

At 11:45, Rocky was at our hole again. Arch was with him, both of them flat out.

"You guys ready?" Rocky glanced at my thumb but said nothing.

We grunted.

"Two things. Do not fall asleep. You fall asleep you'll wake up with your throats slit."

"That's no bullshit," Arch said.

There was a moment's silence.

"What's the other thing?" I asked. Actually, we were whispering, had been whispering for hours, hissing at each other.

"Be sure to get back before dawn. If you're still out there when it's light, you're out there forever."

"You guys sure you're okay?" Arch asked—just to put his two cents in, I thought. Suppose we weren't?

This time only Johnson grunted. Rocky handed a rifle to him. "Give me the BAR," he said. "This is Keaton's M-1. Take care of it. Keaton'll watch over the BAR." That would leave us unencumbered for the night ahead. Rocky was thinking clearly—I mean, when you consider that neither he nor Arch had any more experience with outpost duty than we did. In another moment, after glancing at my thumb again, he was gone, a long thin silhouette bent in half in the moon's baleful light. Arch tailed him, humped over, giving us one last questioning look over his shoulder as though he didn't really trust us. Well, screw him.

I didn't know whether or not I wanted moonlight when we were out there. Would it give us away? Or would it betray the Germans? I had other questions, too, lots of them, but I couldn't seem to get my mind around them. I seemed to have little grasp of things as they actually were; they kept slipping away. Mostly what I had was my fear.

ACTUALLY, when the time came nothing much happened out there. We found the trench easily enough, crawling along side by side, guided by the pile of rubbish nearby, which turned out to be a dead cow, lying alongside its calf, both bloated to double size, but without a stink. We slipped into the hole face-to-face, our legs stretched out almost full-length and the soles of our feet resting flat against each other, as we had been told they would. It was a perfect fit, as though it had been exactly measured to our dimensions. We then tested our alert system by tensing up our bodies and pushing with our feet. We had already decided before we left our foxhole to repeat this exercise every couple of minutes to make sure that we stayed awake. The hole was dug to a perfect depth, allowing us to peer over the top with almost no chance of being seen (although of course we felt visible to the entire world). Johnson faced our lines, I faced the Germans. The idea, as Rocky had told us, was to switch positions midway through our duty, at three o'clock. That exercise would also help to keep us awake.

A couple of hours passed, but when I looked at my watch I saw that it was 12:30. I waited a few minutes and checked again—still 12:30. I understood then, as my blood began to slow, that I would have to spend the rest of the night as a pathetic victim of tedium, that merciless bastard son of time, and that whatever my own human urgencies and needs might be through the long hours, I

had better get used to the idea and learn to accommodate
it. But once again my body was living its own life that night
and had been for hours. I had almost no influence over it.
All I could do was push with the soles of my feet against
Johnson; and Johnson pushed back. That, at least, we
could control; about the rest—the twitching and quivering, the prickling nerves and colonic rumbles—I was
totally helpless.

At last, half the night was gone. It was three o'clock and
still quiet. That was how I wanted it. Johnson and I
changed positions, making a flutter of noise, as we crawled
past each other, that seemed to carry throughout the
whole shallow valley; I thought I heard it echo around us.
Behind me now, as I faced our own lines, I heard creaking
sounds, very faint and slow and erratic. I listened, considered, worried. In the moonlight, which struck Johnson's
face at a sharp, revealing angle, I could see him considering, too. The noise repeated itself, part now of other
sounds. Parsing these sounds, trying to separate them
from one another, I told myself that I heard (1) wheels
creaking, (2) metal cans rattling, and (3) something I
couldn't quite identify but that was definitely related to
the first two. Supply wagons, I guessed, maybe pulled by
horses. (That would be useful information to bring back,
the fact that the German supply wagons were being pulled
by horses.) I pressed Johnson's feet. He pressed back. We
listened together for another fifteen minutes, while the
noises swelled, then dimmed, and finally ceased. An angry
voice shouted something. One word, "*Scheiss.*" The sound
of German, the obscenity spoken in the enemy's voice,
shocked me.

Then all was silent.

Of the five and a half hours that we spent in that first outpost venture, that was the moment of high interest, over in twenty minutes. It was also, I think, the only moment when I wasn't afraid—maybe because I was totally engaged. I wanted to ask Johnson about this when we got back, but I forgot. I wanted to know whether he had felt the same way. By the time we got back, crawling again side by side, eating dirt, and almost missing the critical moment that separates blackness from first light, all the adrenaline had been drained from my body, my memory was gone, and I was curiously uninterested in the whole experience. It seemed to have happened to someone else, some uniformed impostor bearing my name and my features who was passing himself off in the third platoon as me. All I wanted to do was to go to sleep, where I knew—or felt—that upon awakening I would again find my real self.

THE artillery barrages had started, just as Smith said they would. Early morning, before breakfast, and late afternoon. Perfectly regulated, perfectly predictable. Thirty minutes a day, sometimes a little more, paying particular attention to the supply depots that lay a mile or so behind us.

Whump. Whump. Whump.

The aggressive resonance of the German 88's ejaculatory sounds was unique, not duplicated, to my knowledge, by any other artillery piece in World War II. It had the hoarseness of a deadly cough, the baritone echo of thunder, and you could hear it coming.

Whump. Whump. Whump.

Early morning, and late afternoon, with an occasional digressive round or two arched across perhaps in the evening or at noon just so we wouldn't become complacent. Those potshots could be killers.

We respected the 88. It was a formidable gun, with a definite personality of its own. Mobile. Agile. Swift. And accurate. It could bracket a five-hundred-yard ladder—run top to bottom, or the reverse, in half a minute, each exploding rung of the ladder moving ahead with every round. This happened often; it was a favorite German tactic. When it did, the point was to find yourself, flat out, between rungs of the ladder. If you did, and the terrain provided some generous cover, you were generally safe. Or safe enough. There were always exceptions, of course.

Huddled in my foxhole with Johnson, I often got an erection when the shells of the 88s detonated; at the explosion, a panicked rush of blood was released in my groin that was almost Pavlovian in its reliability.

AROUND this time I began to worry about my dog tags. Should I wear them? Should I get rid of them? They bore an "H," for Hebrew, along with my blood type and other essential information. Hebrew was what the US Army had decided to call Jews. I had never been called a Hebrew before. Not even by Hebrews. To the world I had always been a Jew. To myself, as well. Why, then, was a "J" not good enough for the US Army? (Should I have read something into that, something patronizing and offensive?) But I wasn't really worrying about the US Army. I was worrying about the Germans.

What would they do with me if I became a prisoner, when they saw the "H" on my dog tags? What had happened to other "H"s when they were captured?

POW camps, as an American GI, like any other?

Or a German concentration camp, as an "H." *Juden,* as we were known beyond the Rhine—*Juden,* scum of the earth, a phrase I had learned during the thirties from news reports from Germany.

The obvious truth was that all these questions were hypothetical, all the worry mere inner bombast. I couldn't imagine myself without my dog tags, whatever they read. My dog tags were the sole material proof of my identity, so important that they were stamped out of metal to resist destruction, the only external objects I carried that set me apart from everyone else. Without them, who was I? I decided that I would keep them, however threatening the situation. I would be an "H," as the Army insisted. I would defy the Nazis and take my chances, a touch of gratuitous arrogance that I seemed to need to feel at the time.

I FOUND myself wondering then whether Fedderman was also thinking about this, and if so, what he was thinking.

And at the same time, I began to wonder what they had to say to each other—Ira Fedderman and Bern Keaton, chained together in their foxhole—while I was worrying in the silence of my own about my dog tags. Were they discussing Fedderman's problems? About being outsized and physically incompetent; about being an intellectual and an aesthete (a word I learned from Fedderman himself)? Or were they talking about Bern's slow, resistant slide down the slippery chute of secularism, not a happy subject for

PFC Keaton, ex-pupil, as he was, of the nuns of Hacken-sack, New Jersey. (Bern was an intellectual, too, like Fed-derman, but of an especially sweet and modest kind—the rarest kind, in fact, although he would have been surprised to hear it.)

They had plenty to talk about, was my guess; they had a whole world, at least, not like Johnson and me, mumbling our way stuporously through dull two-word exchanges about the necessities of daily life, about food, water, sleep, the noisy state of our cranky bowels, other banal matters.

"Are you okay?" we asked each other a dozen times a day. But not Keaton and Fedderman, I bet. Was I jealous? Yes, I think so. I was jealous because I was lonely. And I never learned what Fedderman thought about being called an "H" because I never got a chance to ask him. It was probably just as well. It was always my conviction that Fedderman had enough to worry about for his own good, without needing more.

"TOUGH shit," Johnson said when I complained about having to live at such close quarters in our trapezoidal hole in the ground. Those were the first words he had spoken since breakfast, and it was now three o'clock in the after-noon. He was not putting me off or defending himself. He was commenting in his strange (to me), disinterested Green Mountain way. I didn't understand disinterested-ness. I'm not even sure I knew the word then. It was emo-tion that I understood, too well, perhaps—emotion and involvement, the more direct the better (although in style I was as cool as the next GI, hoping that my emotions would never be caught out). "Tough shit," when Johnson said it, meant just that; it had no implied reference to me, it made no judgment. Only later, at a time not far off, would I see Johnson involved exactly like everyone else, with passionate emotional force, and that time would be a sad one for all of us.

I never learned what Vermont town Johnson came from, what his family did to support themselves, where he had gone to school, what his prejudices and ambitions were, his likes and dislikes. I wondered then—and still do— whether he himself knew about his prejudices and ambitions. In place of real information, he offered a thin-lipped reticence, which had become a stony presence in itself— the Johnson presence, tight-assed and tense, that gave nothing away. I think he was even shy with himself.

But my complaint was real. The hole had become crowded with personal trash. The mud didn't help. Neither did the smell. Our sweaty bodies, rarely washed. Stained underwear, as soiled today as yesterday, and unchanged. Our excrement, a daily problem, never solved. All the sour run-off of ordinary life. None of it could be avoided.

I lost control of myself then, as I had when I ran off during maneuvers in Tennessee, and again there was no warning. Late one afternoon, I leapt out of our hole, dropped my pants, and squatted on the ground six feet away. It was a kind of metabolic impulse, irresistible and even exhilarating. I remember, as I squatted there, objectively wondering how various the world can suddenly appear when you shift your angle of vision, even minimally. The plain in front of me suddenly broadened as though it covered all of Alsace, the shallow ridges seemed to run as far to the east as I could see, and there was a whole new world, it seemed, of thorny brush and dun-colored hills out there, glinting in the afternoon sun. Even the sky itself, as I looked up, seemed to open.

"Jesus Christ!" Bern yelled. "Get back where you belong!"

I looked at him, a few feet away. I felt sorry for him. Poor Bern, stuck in his man-made foxhole, how could he understand how I felt? Alongside Bern, Fedderman sat with his back to me, his hands covering his eyes. I guess he figured, like me, if he didn't see it, it wasn't happening. I shook my head in sympathy. Then there was the strange assaultive sound of a rifle shot nearby, and a bullet hit the ground a few feet behind me, plowing the dirt. For me? I wondered, not yet as serious as I should have been.

"Jesus!" Bern yelled again.

I looked ahead from my squatting position, shielding my eyes with the flat of my hand. I could see a German soldier, visible from the waist up, standing inside one of the folds in the hills ahead of us, a couple of hundred yards away. He was wearing a green overcoat with a high collar and enormous padded shoulders, and he was bareheaded; no cap, no helmet, which somehow made him seem unmistakably German. Also, I saw, he was laughing. All this was very clear to me: his laughter, the details of his clothing, the padded shoulders, the high collar, the bare head. I even thought that I could see his teeth. But in another second, I began to move, slowly at first, a hesitant reflex. Then there was another shot and another clear miss. The dirt flew again. But this time I was on my feet, holding on to my pants, and in another second I was in our foxhole, where Johnson sat looking at me impassively.

"Why doesn't somebody shoot the son of a bitch?" I asked him, buckling up. Of course there was no answer. I really couldn't get over that. My buddies, where were they? What were they thinking?

Anyway, I began to laugh. I had to. To save my foolish face, to acknowledge that I was still alive. The game was over. I believe the son of a bitch deliberately chose to miss me with his two shots. I believe that he just wanted a little late afternoon sport, to relieve the general tedium, and I happened to be it. Maybe I wanted the same thing.

I still think of that bareheaded Kraut from time to time, laughing like that. I wonder whether he survived the war, and, if he did, what his life was like afterward. I would be curious to know about that. I also wonder if he ever thinks of me and in what terms. Is he still laughing?

THAT night, the second outpost venture for Johnson and me, there was another game, a new one. This game consisted of the Germans shouting provocative remarks at us—through bullhorns—at regular intervals for a period of about two hours, while Johnson and I sat sole-to-sole in our slit trench. Some of these remarks were obscene, others were subversive. At least that seemed to be the intention. All, however, were crazed, in what was for the moment the German way—crazed and curiously half-hearted.

"Your beloved leader, Mrs. Rosenfeldt, is a Chew." Repeated many times, in heavily accented English, with simpleminded variations. Each time I heard it, I touched my dog tags.

"Your sweethearts at home, your darlings, are being fucked by *schwarze*-blacks, yes?" Did that "yes" express a doubt or merely a weird politeness?

"While you eat shit from tin cans, your family at home eats steak." Bull's-eye.

"Babe Ruth is a *schwarz*-black Chew. Did you know that?"

"New York was wiped out by Cherman bombers. The Statue of Liberty is no more. *Kaputt. Alles kaputt.*"

I guess all this was supposed to keep the men on the line in an edgy state. But it also had to keep the Germans just as edgy. To what end? Could they be serious about us? About the Yankee Division? About the softness of our morale? About Babe Ruth, Mrs. Rosenfeldt, the Statue of Liberty?

To the credit of the 104th regiment, little, to my knowledge, was ever made of the hectoring by the German Army that night, or any other night. It was treated as though it was beneath contempt, a sub-human aberration, a joke in bad taste. Motherfucking Krauts, was the general and silent attitude; they must be at the end of their motherfucking rope. Beyond the pale, not like us.

THE NEXT morning, Rocky was gone. He had disappeared overnight, at some indeterminate hour before the Germans had launched their hopeless episode of psychological warfare. Barney Barnato himself brought the news, appearing on his stomach at the edge of our hole, while Johnson and I were still drinking our morning coffee, recovering from outpost duty. Barney had crawled the ten-yard patch between us breathing hard from excitement, with an I-knew-it-all-the-time look on his face, to ask us if we had seen our squad leader.

Johnson's eyes opened wide at the question. I saw a tremor go through him. As I've said before and still say, nobody was more essential to the first squad than Rocky Hubbell.

"The last I saw of him," I said, refusing to show Barney any emotion, "was last night when Fedderman and Keaton brought rations up."

"You're sure, now?"

"That's when I last saw him." Setting my jaw and looking away.

It was true. Around eight or so the previous evening, Fedderman and Keaton were approaching our lines with a load of K rations they had picked up in the rear—regulation duty—when they were caught in a surprise 88 ladder barrage. They began to run toward us when they realized what was happening—whump, whump, whump—and in another moment the concussion of an exploding shell had blown them both off their feet and scattered the load of rations. That's all it took, a moment. Fedderman and Keaton flew into the air—in slow motion, it seemed—and came down hard. I saw the look of amazement on Fedderman's face when this happened, just like my own, a stop-frame of shock and fear that lasted hardly a second. In another moment, dozens of K ration boxes littered the ground around us and when the 88 quieted down a minute later, we all rushed out of our holes, like scavengers, to gather in the stuff. Put simply, we were looting. Brewster and Natale, too, crawled around like the rest of us—"B and N," as we had come to call them. By then, Bern had picked himself up and was reverently touching his body, as though looking for a consoling wound somewhere.

"You all right?" I shouted.

He nodded his head yes and kept poking at his body. Meanwhile, as the rest of us raced around picking up boxes, Rocky was comforting Fedderman, who was sitting on the ground, looking bleary-eyed—looking, in fact, drunk.

"Give me a hand," Rocky said, in his benign way, and I stopped what I was doing and tried to help him lift Fedderman by the armpits, then by the waist, feeling the flab, the stomach roll, the oily fleshiness that he had some-how managed to hold on to through all the months of our training.

"You've got to help me," I said to Fedderman. "I can't do it by myself." I suddenly seemed to be alone with my old pal.

As I spoke, his eyes rolled up into his head, his head fell forward, and his body went slack. "Somebody!" I called, feeling panic for the first time.

"What?" It was Willis, looking down at me, carrying a dozen K ration boxes.

"I don't know whether Fedderman's alive."

Willis put down his boxes and knelt on the ground alongside me, taking his time. He lifted Fedderman's left eyelid and peered at his eyeball.

"He fainted," Willis said. "Probably concussed. Hold him up."

While I bent over behind Fedderman and held him under the armpits, Willis slapped him hard on each cheek with the flat of his hand. He made quite a sound doing it, as though he was delivering an important message that must be heard. I winced at each blow. "Don't make such a face," Willis said to me. "I know what I'm doing."

But so, of course, did the Germans who, sighting this inviting little cluster that the first squad had made, against all rules, began to lob in a mortar shell here and there—

not, however, with much accuracy. But it instantly re-established a sense of reality. While the Germans tried to find the range, we made for our holes, Willis and Bern between them dragging Fedderman, who was just opening his eyes.

None of us realized that Rocky had disappeared while we were trying to revive Fedderman, just when dusk was dissolving into night, just at the moment when Paul Willis assumed such authority. None of us gave Rocky a thought that night. He was the squad leader. We rarely questioned him and rarely doubted. Rocky did pretty much what he wanted, and we had learned to hope for the best. We assumed that he was in his foxhole; I don't know what Willis and Barney were thinking.

And so Barney Barnato showed up the next morning on his belly, slithering toward us like a snake, to spread the news. Somehow the story made Barney happy.

"I knew he'd pull something like this sooner or later," Barney said, unable to keep from grinning, although the tone of his voice was serious enough, and remembering the sound of Willis's flat palm on Fedderman's cheeks, I wanted to slap Barney in exactly the same way.

"Pull what?" I asked, setting my jaw again.

"A trick like this," Barney said, trying to stare me down.

"Maybe he's on special duty," I said. That sounded stupidly loyal, even to me. But I didn't know what to think. What should I have thought? That Rocky had deserted to the enemy? My imagination had blocked; I could think of nothing. But Barney was already crawling away, uninterested in any other opinions from me, to spread the news to Bern and Fedderman, who had apparently slept off his "concussion" while the Germans were assaulting us through the night with their obscenities.

Later in the morning, we had a quick visit from Lieutenant Gallagher, accompanied by Arch, who looked unhappy.

"What do you guys know?" Gallagher asked, dropping into our hole with us. (Arch lay on his stomach alongside, listening.) This put us at close quarters with an officer, face-to-face; a rare occurrence. It made me shy. Gallagher, too, I thought. We both seemed to be feeling powerfully the difference in rank between us at that moment. I hadn't realized how pointy Gallagher's teeth were until he was directly in front of me; his face, too, was like a tamed ferret's. I could see each pore around his nostrils, each tiny aerated depression. Quick brown eyes, a zit on the side of his neck. Don't come any closer, I thought. Keep your distance. Sir. Up close like that, he kept showing us his sharp little incisors when he smiled. I tried to concentrate on them, but Gallagher didn't smile often that morning. I didn't think he had slept much the night before, like Johnson and me. I wasn't happy with this visit.

I'll say it again: I really liked Gallagher. We all did. I can't say that enough. I had the feeling that he never lied, especially to himself. (I wanted to be like that.) Also, I knew that he treated everybody in exactly the same way— I mean everybody. And, far more rare than you might think, he didn't compete with his men in the third platoon, did not compete with them, malign them, laugh at them, or condescend, as we saw all around us all the time in other platoons, in other companies. Rocky had once said, "Don't worry your asses about F. J. Gallagher. He's not a

man who will leave his wounded on the battlefield."
Starchy words, maybe, but as soon as Rocky spoke them, I
felt the truth of what he had just said. I also thought they
might serve just as well for Rocky. I hoped so. I wanted
both of them to be great.

So there we were in the hole, maybe six inches from
each other, one officer and two PFCs, while Arch listened
in, resting uncomfortably on his belly. "Well?" Gallagher
asked. He was pretending to fool with his carbine so we
wouldn't have to look each other in the eye. PFCs never
looked officers in the eye; they only stared. "You know,"
Gallagher said, "Antonovich is really pissed off." Not Captain Antonovich, just Antonovich, as though he was anybody. "It's one thing in the States, Rocky's little escapades,
but up here . . ." As though we were on the moon.

"You got me," I said, stupid again. Oh, how I wanted to
sound intelligent, to speak all-knowing words to the lieutenant that would solve the mystery of Rocky Hubbell's
disappearance.

"Pissed off is only the half of it," Arch put in, from his
peculiar position.

Gallagher turned to him wearily. "Rest, sergeant," he
said, with an irony you could heft in the palm of your
hand. "Now," Gallagher went on, but only to Johnson and
me, "no clues? Nothing he said? Nothing strange in the
way he acted? Think, fellows, because if he's deserted . . ."

At his words, I was swept away by deep gloom. Deser-
tion. The barrenness of the word, its heavy sobriety, its
endlessness: it was one of those words that seemed to go
on forever. But Rocky Hubbell a deserter? There was a
missed connection somewhere. That's all it was, a missed
connection.

"There's no way Rocky would desert," I said.

"Swear on it," Gallagher answered, as unexpectedly sarcastic as Fedderman could be. This reply pulled me up a bit. I could feel his seriousness and his doubts; and of course he was right. Part of his job was to be serious and skeptical. By then, Gallagher had settled into our hole and I began to suspect that he didn't want to leave. "How well do you know him?" he asked.

I hesitated. "Well enough," I said.

Gallagher nodded approvingly. "And the rest of the squad?"

"You mean how well do I know them?"

"Yes."

Again I hesitated. "Well enough, too, I guess." I didn't know what he was getting at.

"Got anything to say, Johnson?"

Johnson shook his head.

Lieutenant Gallagher kept twitching the corners of his mouth back, as though he was doing an exercise. Those incisors looked like dog's teeth from six inches away. I wanted him to leave. I wasn't used to having conversations like this. How well did I know Rocky Hubbell and the rest of the first squad? Or anybody else in C Company, for that matter. I didn't know Roger Johnson; I recognized that a long time ago. But I knew Bern Keaton (so I flattered myself). I knew that Bern Keaton had a girlfriend named Sheila who lived in Passaic, New Jersey, near his hometown of Hackensack, and that Bern had grown up in a wood-shingle house, much like my own in Baltimore. I also knew about the religious thing. And maybe I knew a thing or two about Ira Fedderman. Ira Fedderman had a sister named Naomi. He had let that slip once, but never talked about it again. His father, whose name was Julius, was a housepainter in Bensonhurst, Brooklyn. And yes, there was more. I knew that Paul Willis stole his buddies' underwear and Barney Barnato always saw the worst in everyone, as though he was all too familiar with the worst. And George Brewster, amazing us with his candor, had once remarked that given a choice between sexual intercourse and a really satisfying bowel movement, he was not at all sure that he would take sexual intercourse. He actually said that; and he didn't say "fucking," he said "sexual intercourse."

But Arch and Antonovich and Gallagher and the rest? We were a company of strangers, still unknown to each other. Maybe it was enough to admire Gallagher, as I did.

"Antonovich wants Rocky's ass, and for once I don't blame him," Gallagher said, sounding sad. Those were his last words to us. "Let's go, sergeant," he said to Arch. And they were off.


TRUE to his nature and all his past behavior, Rocky showed up late in the afternoon, just before our second 88 barrage of the day was due to begin. (The Germans' regularity helped to regulate us.) He sauntered toward us looking seven feet tall from where we sat in our hole. He was unshaved, but he was often unshaved. He had a self-satisfied smile on his face, as though he knew a few things we didn't know; we were familiar with that smile. When he got to Bern and Fedderman's hole, he pulled out a handgun and pointed it at them as though it was a street holdup or a bank robbery. Fedderman's eyes bulged when he saw the gun. Then he began to laugh dutifully, along with Bern. They knew what to do. When Rocky turned away and headed for us, hunched over a little (the first 88 shell had landed a couple of hundred yards behind us), Bern began to frantically tap his temple with his forefinger. Nuts, was the message. Rocky Hubbell was nuts.

When Rocky pointed the handgun at Johnson and me, we didn't laugh. There was nothing funny about it— nothing friendly, either. It was just a tall Texas jerk, who had once been the perfect squad leader, standing over us, acting like a jerk. It was just a crazy stunt. The gun was a Luger, Rocky told us, suddenly sounding self-conscious. The German Army's finest. (I was not interested in the German Army's finest.) He had picked up the revolver overnight, he went on, in the company of a couple of other desperadoes, old renegade pals from B Company, old caper buddies from the States, along with several other mementos, including an officer's sword from World War I, still in its sheath, which was now officially in the possession of B Company. What they had to do to acquire their new possessions, he did not describe. But it had been quite a night, he said, a wild foray in search of gratuitous glory.

After Rocky spoke those fancy words, he waited for our response. There was none. Rocky wanted us to tell him how wonderful he had been—how brave and impressive; how free-spirited—while our lives and a few other lives, all the lives in the first squad, were at risk as Johnson and I had sweated it out on outpost during his absence.

It all happened in the neighborhood of Looney-ville, Rocky said, near where the Seventh Army was dug in on our flank. (In reality, the Seventh Army was dug in farther north.) He and his cronies had borrowed a vehicle for the trip. Then Rocky waited again, and waited some more, for a few words from us, but we weren't interested. We had no questions. Let Antonovich and Gallagher ask the questions. Or somebody else who was interested in Rocky. He had lost us. It was one caper too many.

The prick.

# SEVEN

# The Horseshoe

BY FIRST daylight, which appeared as a thin, milk-white streak that barely stretched across the horizon, I was face down in the mud, sprawled out at least fifteen feet from my nearest buddy, Roger Johnson. Johnson was also face down, also sprawled out, with the BAR we shared dizzily upended a few yards to his right, as though he had thrown it away, hurled it with all his strength in a sudden panic. The tripod that supported the muzzle was missing one leg, and the muzzle itself was stuck in the mud. Johnson was making strange noises again, pulling at his bandoleers. He was speaking a language I had never heard before, making it up as he lay there face down in the mud. Panic was everywhere that morning.

Bern Keaton lay flat out on the other side of Johnson, a couple of yards farther on, in position exactly as the other assistant BAR man. He was trying to say something to Johnson, maybe to me, too, but I couldn't hear him against the rattling din of machine-gun fire, which emptied my head and, for the moment, smashed all my sensory perceptions. But then I could see Bern's helmet, with the straps hanging loose, against all regulations, his head bobbing inside. He always let his straps hang loose; he was notorious for it. It drove Arch and Antonovich crazy.

The rest of the squad—and the rest of the third platoon, as well—was spread-eagled on the ground in sloppy combat formation. Fedderman was positioned somewhere ahead of Bern, where he had fallen at the first salvo, like the rest of us, looking like a bloated loaf of bread as he lay there. Willis and Barnato were somewhere to their right, alongside both Brewster and Natale, who remained inseparable even in the worst crisis. Rocky was way ahead of us and no longer in sight, probably already on the other side of the rise, too far out in front. This was unforgivable, in my opinion—to lose contact with the squad, to separate himself from us like that.


ROCKY had awakened us at 5 a.m. in our foxhole, hissing dim orders into our ears. Something about attack formation, something about the whole third platoon, plus a few extras from other units, moving out together. I could hardly see him, kneeling alongside us. I didn't want to see him as he whispered to us in the dark. But Johnson and I listened carefully. Rocky was telling us that we were going to attack those shallow rises that lay in front of us. We were really going to move out against them, as we had always suspected. For a second only, as Rocky hissed at us, a terrifying paralysis came over me, then lifted. Johnson was making snorting noises again, and I was coughing, belching, farting—all the percussive effects of fear sounding off as one. In another moment, Rocky was gone to take the news to Bern and Fedderman, and soon we quieted down and began to wait in silence.

When the platoon gathered a half-hour later, as ordered, the word was passed along to form a diamond formation. We did as we were told, shuffling around clumsily, taking our time and colliding with each other, as though we weren't entirely in control of ourselves. We could barely see under the dim moon, and we were deliberately dragging our feet. So were the other squads. Rocky hissed at us to move our asses, to watch what we were doing, to be quiet, until he finally had us in formation, or as close as he would ever get us. From tip to tip, once it was shaped, the third platoon's diamond probably extended for about fifty yards. We rested then on our feet and waited until the first light was almost up. While we waited, a kind of self-imposed boredom set in, a familiar rigidity of the senses that was like putting blinders on to shut out the world, pretty much what always happened when we were scared shitless. As we were that morning, waiting there to move out.

Then Gallagher stepped out of the shadows, high-stepping in front of us like a nervous colt, at the very point of the diamond, as he prepared to lead us in attack formation out of the little Alsatian valley we had been occupying and to herd us up the slight rise that climbed in folds in front of our lines. We moved behind him sluggishly, slowed by inertia and terror, the diamond losing its pristine shape almost immediately. Close it up, Fedderman, I wanted to yell. And you, too, Johnson, and Bern, and all the rest. We climbed slowly, positioned almost midway along the diamond's length, barely feeling the ascent.

The folds of the rise, I could now see, were roughly shaped like a horseshoe, with the curve narrowly facing in our direction. What Rocky told us when we started was that we were expected to straighten out the curve, force it back so that it would no longer poke into our territory and threaten us. There was no discussion of tactics. There were barely any orders. There wasn't time. We assumed, if we assumed anything, that our squad leaders had been filled in.

The third platoon continued to move out, still climbing slowly, still wearing a mask of false boredom like a shield, half-blind with fear.

WITHIN a few moments, in terrible confusion, in a situation that was no longer comprehensible, a lot had happened. Lieutenant Gallagher, for one, was already dead. We saw him die, quickly. A bullet pierced his scrawny boy's neck, with its enlarged Adam's apple and its zit, as he moved forward ahead of us, just over the top of the rise. I heard shouting, maybe the sound of my own voice, or Bern's or Fedderman's. Someone yelled *Kaputt!* as though it was an order. Gallagher stood there, upright and motionless, his ferret's face full of surprise, when the Germans began to fire their Mausers. At the same moment, perfectly synchronized, a 180-degree sweep of machine-gun fire, which at first I mistook for our own, took us from right to left, along the horseshoe's curve, dropping the platoon where it stood. It then came around in a second sweep. It was that sweep that smashed me.

I saw a hole open up in the back of Lieutenant Gallagher's neck when the bullet passed through from the front—surprised at how large and black it was, clean, too, as though it had been drilled by a mechanic's precision tool. There was a surge of surface blood at first, then a gurgle, like a tap being turned on, then a sudden torrent as he fell without a sound. Both of his carotid arteries must have poured in one stream through the wound. All of this took perhaps a dozen seconds: Gallagher's death, the machine-gun assault, and the paralysis of the third platoon.

We lay on the ground without moving. It was now light. This was when Bern tried to say something to Johnson and maybe to me, too, but I couldn't hear him. I remember from that moment, when mass disorientation began to set in, the glob-smell of mud in my nostrils. I remember, too, the sudden drying up of saliva in my mouth and the instant dehydration it produced; the powerful feel of my own body, as though I was carrying it as a burden; my skinny, attenuated frame, lying there on the ground, waiting; the heavy presence of limbs extending from it; my helmeted skull, quivering torso, and vulnerable crotch, the tender genitals curled dead-center at my pelvis; and my swollen bladder, burning. The sounds, too, never before heard, swelling over the noise of small-arms and machine-gun fire, of men's voices calling for help or screaming in pain or terror—our own men's voices, unrecognizable at first, weird in pitch and timbre. And the hum inside my own head, just as weird and unfamiliar, buzzing furiously, trying to drown out the sounds coming from all around me.

In that moment, also, Johnson was calling for water, moaning as though he was about to lose consciousness. Natale, lying alongside Brewster, was cursing and vomiting and drawing fire with his cries. There was nothing from the rest of the squad. I didn't know where Rocky was. He was too far in front. By then, he was probably dead. The other voices—from the rest of the platoon and the extras from another unit, scattered everywhere—I hardly recognized.


ALMOST without a pause, the German machine-gun fire segued into mortar explosions, then suddenly stopped. Mortar shells began to drop into the middle of our pathetic diamond, spraying shrapnel on all sides: large jagged metal jigsaws, tiny needle-splinters, chunky steel rocks whinging outward. But the range was apparently short, too short for accuracy, and the damage to us mostly accidental. When they finished with the mortars, the Germans began to lob grenades; these, too, fell inside the diamond but they were more effective than the mortars. Grenades were very accurate within their limited range. They were to draw blood all day long.

Finally, I discovered—we all discovered, those of us who still lived—the chilling new presence of snipers, whose main job was to pick off our wounded: easy work that day, for each target was already immobilized. Nothing was neglected by the Germans in the face of our elephantine approach. They responded with lethal efficiency. And the Germans—who remained invisible in their positions, as they half-surrounded us on the curve of the horseshoe—had all the time in the world to play with us. It was cushioned time, too, as it turned out, for there was no response that day from the rest of C Company behind us, no answering artillery or heavy weapons fire, and no supporting troops to help us slip out of the horseshoe rise that we had trapped ourselves in. The company hung tight somewhere in the rear for reasons of its own, never explained by Captain Antonovich or Master Sergeant Archambault, both of whom had somehow managed to escape this trip. I thought of them bitterly and cursed them both for pigs.

Slowly then, as the morning wore on and the knowledge began to sink in, I came to realize that for us there was nothing to do but wait, flat out as we were, for our own deaths.

WITHIN minutes of Lieutenant Gallagher's death, I began to play the corpse. It was the only option. I tried to freeze my muscles and nerves first, concentrating as though it was a yoga exercise. Then I allowed myself a single diminished breath every fifteen seconds or so, sometimes longer, increasingly longer, until I felt my heartbeat and pulse slow. Soon I was able to keep the rhythm of my breathing steady and my limbs from trembling. In that way, I hoped to make myself invisible. I imagined—I had to imagine—that I was actually shrinking from sight as I lay there, that no one could see me and that, unseen, I would be safe.

That is how I went on for hours, playing the living corpse, beginning to believe, at odd moments, that I might really be dead and already in a transitory state, and occasionally distracting myself, in a purely nervous, hallucinatory reflex, by pretending to slip out of my body as I waited for the end so that I could detachedly observe my own sodden form from above, cringing and shriveled into itself in the mud below. An awful sight.

.  .  .

OUT OF my peripheral vision, I glimpsed a body suddenly rise to its feet and race for the rear, followed by a quick burst of machine-gun fire. The body disappeared, the firing ceased. Paul Willis? Barney Barnato? I couldn't tell, and I would never know. By then, fifteen feet away, Johnson was begging for water, whimpering softly into the mud without stopping—an animal's sound that came from deep in his larynx, with no recognizable human overtones. It was not possible to help him. That I swear. It was not possible to help anyone. Ralph Natale, alongside Brewster, was convulsing from his wounds. Ira Fedderman, somewhere ahead of Bern, whose helmet I could no longer see, was calling for his mother, the saddest call of all. So were others. Rocky was gone, on the other side of the ridge, too far in front. I was no longer sure where Bern was. If Fedderman and Natale would only shut up. And all the rest. I continued to breathe quietly, without motion, in that diminished way. I began to count slowly, to soothe myself. I watched myself from above. I probably was crying.

AROUND noon, I heard the rattle of a plane overhead, the buzz of an old engine. It stayed around for a couple of minutes, hovering above us, then disappeared to the south, to our rear. I kept listening for it long after it vanished. Nothing came of it.

BY EARLY afternoon, my canteen had opened up a sore on my hip, from the abrasive pressure that came from lying still. I could feel the sore begin to ooze. It burned, but it offered a distraction I could concentrate on. I didn't mind.

. . .

THE DAY edged on. I could only guess at the time.

At one point, I heard commands being given in German, loud and confident-sounding, but also harried and urgent. An exchange followed, then more commands. Maybe it meant that the Germans had decided to pack up and move out—a foolish judgment. In a little while, there was another round of machine-gun fire, then quiet, then one or two mortar shells, more quiet, then grenades and sniper fire. Sniper fire pretty much all the time—the pattern, the routine, perfectly regulated for the rest of the day, but at a far slower pace as the hours wore on.

STILL, through it all, I remained untouched; I lived, safe in my levitating body, barely breathing, never moving. Not even when Natale, sprawled alongside Brewster maybe ten yards away, died with one final heave, still convulsing.

And where was Bern? Who had tried to escape to the rear? And why was Johnson no longer whimpering? And when would Fedderman shut up? The noise he made, choking from asthma and terror, calling for his mother. And the noise all the others made . . .

More time passed.

HOURS later, toward dusk, when everything was in shadow and the air had noticeably chilled, the medics arrived. I heard them before I saw them, moving around carrying stretchers and speaking in whispers. I had a charge of adrenaline then, before stirring into action. That

was what their unexpected arrival did for me. It brought
me to life.

I dared to move a limb, then another, shifting my legs to
the right. Nothing happened. There was no machine-gun
fire, no mortar shells, no grenades, no snipers. This worried me for a moment. I looked for a trick. Had the Germans actually pulled back? Or were they still in position,
waiting to pick the rest of us off? I moved again. An arm
this time, both legs again, calamitously stiff, then my
head. I had the beginnings of a leg cramp; a contraction
moved from my calf straight up through my thigh. I knew
what was coming and how painful it would be. The medics
were poking around, looking for wounded bodies. There
were not many on that rise. The medics had not yet seen
me, or I them. But I heard them and I felt them nearby,
poking around. The light was fading fast. Shadows were
now black. We had been trapped for twelve hours, and it
was very quiet. I didn't want the medics to miss me. I
wanted them to know that I was there. I called something
to them and got to my knees.

"Don't move." A soft voice answering, full of anxiety.

I looked up. A clean young man was standing over me.
He wore an armband with a red cross on it and carried no
weapon. "Don't move," he said again.

"Is it over?" I asked.

"We think it's over," he said. "It better be over. Are you
all right?"

"I have a leg cramp."

"No wounds?"

"No."

"Don't play the hero," he said. He kept glancing over his
shoulder as though he expected to be attacked. "Which leg?"

I had been quietly moaning to myself as my muscles contracted. And now my other foot was asleep. I knelt there, waiting for the circulation to return, the muscles to relax. Now the moaning was involuntary.

"I don't know that there's anything I can do about a leg cramp," the medic said.

"Tell me what's going on."

Two of the medics passed us then, carrying a body on a stretcher. They were slipping in the mud and trying to keep their balance. I didn't recognize the face on the stretcher—somebody half-familiar, I thought, from another squad. Then, in another moment, the cramp was gone, a surge of unexpected energy suddenly went through me—perhaps the absolute last of my adrenaline—and I leapt up, touching myself everywhere, genitals first. Then I took a full minute to piss.

What I think I wanted to do was look for Bern Keaton, but I was afraid, and it was dark; we were all becoming black silhouettes on the battleground. Where would I look?

The medic was checking dog tags on some of the bodies, peering at them as he yanked them out of their shirtfronts. "We'll get this mess cleaned up by midnight," he said.

I knew he meant the dead.

Without an exchange, I began to help the medic with a stretcher holding somebody from the third squad. I didn't know his name. He looked dead to me—comfortable and slack from where I stood. Part of his lower jaw was missing, on the left side. One of the other medics was pouring some powder into the wound. The guy from the third squad didn't move, didn't flinch. I wanted to tell the medic that he was dead, that the powder was useless, but I kept quiet. They were the experts, they were the medics. I only knew how to fire a BAR and an M-1, under certain favorable conditions.

The medic counted to three. "Now," he said, and we picked the stretcher up. It didn't weigh a lot but it felt lumpy. I still thought the guy was dead. In fact, I was sure of it. It was the lumpiness, as though there was no center of gravity to the body, as though the corpse was made up of nothing but pulpy tentacles. Then we were off to the rear, moving slowly as a few stars appeared in the east and evening really began to shield us. I felt invulnerable in that darkness. I was no longer afraid, and for a couple of seconds I was in a state of near-exaltation. The adrenaline again, I guessed. I tried to hold on to the feeling, but it didn't last. We moved on. I was dragging my feet and telling myself, as fear began to return, that everything that could happen had already happened.

There was no more firing. The whole small valley, the horseshoe itself, was silent. I told myself that the Germans must have pulled back. They must have had enough for one day. And why not? They had won a splendid victory.


IT WAS a long trip. My cramped leg hurt. My hip-sore burned and I wanted a cigarette. By the time we got back to company headquarters, perhaps five hundred yards to the rear, I was visibly trembling.

"You're shaking," the medic said.

I couldn't stop. The medic said it again, and I waved him off. "It's just from carrying the stretcher," I said.

Soon we were loading it onto a jeep for the journey back to the division hospital. Another jeep had left about ten minutes earlier, the driver said. I wanted to make the trip, too, as though I had been respectably wounded, something in the thigh, a piece of hot metal in the fleshy part. But I was intact and unbloodied, and a little contemptuous of myself for it.

There were troops hanging around, I saw, maybe a couple of platoons lined up in the dark. They stood there in silence, shifting from one foot to the other. I thought they were staring at me. Were they getting ready to head back to the horseshoe, to occupy it? Were they going to try to fill the gap left in the lines by the disappearance of the third platoon? Whichever, I thought, it was tough shit for them, and their faces showed that they knew it, too.

I soon discovered where Antonovich had spent the day. I found him inside company headquarters' tent, standing in front of a table, facing me. He was as clean as a whistle. His field phone was off the hook, and he was blowing his nose violently. Then he hung up the phone. There were papers all over the place, as though someone had thrown them in the air and then let them rest wherever they landed. When Antonovich saw me, he began to moan. It was a terrible sound to hear coming from an officer.

"Sweet Jesus," he moaned, waving his hands in front of his face, as though he was trying to erase me.

There was some movement in the tent. I saw the commanding officers of A and B Companies standing by, looking embarrassed. There were a couple of lieutenants hanging around, too, pretending that nothing was happening.

"Sweet Jesus," Antonovich moaned. "Get this man's name down. Somebody." His voice rose. But he wouldn't

look at me. "What's your name, soldier? Never mind, I
know your name. K something, right? Put this man in for
a silver star. I want that in the records, in writing. I want it
in C Company's record. Tell me your name again, soldier.
Ah, sweet Jesus." And so on and on, for a while, looking
away, blocking me from his sight.

Antonovich's hysteria never failed him. His face was
streaked with it, as though someone on the other team had
just smashed him in the face with a football. His eyes were
slitted, too, which was unusual for him—either to keep
the world out at that moment or himself in.

"Just get me out of here," I finally said.

I hardly recognized my voice. I could barely find it. I
thought I was speaking in normal tones, maybe even a little softer than usual. But I was no less hysterical than
Michael Antonovich, and the hysteria must have streaked
my face, too. I must have looked wild—wild and filthy and
mud-scummed. I realized that I was scaring everyone. I
was the unwanted guest. Antonovich and his buddies from
A and B Companies were clearly planning something big.
They were in the middle of their own drama, I was sure,
trying to decide how to salvage the disaster of the horseshoe, and I had interrupted them. Then I discovered that
Arch was in the tent, too, cowering silently in a corner.
That was how I saw him: cowering. I turned away. I
wouldn't look at him. Arch and I were finished. Let him
despair. Antonovich and Archambault. What a team. I
knew they wished I would just disappear.

A few other figures came clear. There was some major
hanging around, somebody I had never seen before, with
his oak leaves pasted to his shoulder as though he was a
tree, somebody from battalion or regiment. He was flog-

ging himself on the thigh with a short stout stick, looking angry but not saying a word. Keeping an eye on all of us were two stupid-looking MPs, standing ominously on guard at the entrance to the tent as though they were not going to let anyone escape.

At least I was clean for this audience. I hadn't pissed my pants. I hadn't shat myself. I hadn't run away, either. I had stayed with my buddies (as if there were a choice). I was a winner, all right. I had seen it in Arch's fish-eyes. I could read it there. I could see it in all the others, too: in Antonovich, in the two captains, in the angry major, the MPs, the whole ragtag staff. A winner. They couldn't wait to get rid of me. Then I left on my own steam, while the phone began to squawk on Antonovich's desk.

When I got outside, I finally lighted up—my first smoke since dawn—and almost fainted when I inhaled. The clean young medic who was waiting for me had to hold me up, that's how dizzy I was. It didn't last long, only for a few seconds.


I LANDED at the division hospital an hour later, riding in the jeep alongside the guy from the third squad. The driver took a good look at him before we started and rolled his eyes at the medic. "Do your best," the medic said, shrugging. Then I thanked the medic, and he shrugged a second time. I never saw him again.

On the way, an 88 ladder barrage caught us on the road, and the driver and I, without exchanging a word, left our wounded charge on top of the jeep, wholly exposed, and ran for decent cover at the side of the road. That's what we did. Later, when the barrage was over, we found our ward

just as we had left him, untouched. But I couldn't look the
driver in the eye.

A Catholic chaplain greeted us as we drove into the hospital base by making the sign of the cross over the jeep.
When he did that, something broke inside of me and I
began to cry. The chaplain said something resonant in
Latin and made the sign of the cross again, his hands
sweeping gracefully over the three of us this time. I continued to cry and didn't stop until they stuck a needle in
my arm and finally put me to sleep. But first they had to
cut my right boot off because my foot was so swollen from
the cold and the wet; the left came off easily enough,
almost by itself.

# EIGHT

## Base Hospital

WHEN I woke up the next day, I learned that Bern Keaton and Roger Johnson had both passed through the base hospital an hour or so before I arrived and were already on their way to the UK. It was a thrilling piece of news, just what I needed then—the knowledge that they lived. Bern, I was told, had been shot through the left foot and needed an operation. Johnson had a wound in his upper arm, of the kind, apparently, that I had longed for myself—serious enough but not too serious. The guy from the third squad, with the missing jaw, was dead. He was dead when he arrived—dead, probably, before we left for the base hospital from company headquarters on our open jeep. And that was it, the whole roll call.

So there were three survivors from the third platoon: Bern Keaton, Roger Johnson, and me, our own little cluster of BAR men. It was almost too neat, too contained, as though the three of us, while occupying a certain small triangle on one side of the horseshoe, had been set apart—

by luck, geography, God knows what else—as a chosen few. All we were missing was Ira Fedderman, who, as I also learned that morning, was dead with the rest of them— close to forty in all, although I was never able to learn the exact figure—back on those small hills.

I WAS something new in the Yankee Division, a combat survivor, a prime specimen, and I soon discovered that important people at the base hospital were interested in talking to me. The division's historian wanted to talk to me. The division's psychiatrist also wanted to talk to me, and in fact was already tailing me around the base while I was having the first exchanges with the historian. Two competitors, clearly. They both lived by hearsay, of course, through other people's stories, other people's lives; that was how their professions were defined. And each one wanted something else from me, on his own terms and for his own territory.

HIST.: Tell me again what happened, private.

I was a private first class, not a private, but I didn't correct him. It would make no difference anyway; it was only a nuance of rank. Instead, I grew stubborn. I told him again what happened, for the second time, becoming more and more excited as I talked. Excited to the point of throwing up at his feet, which humiliated me.

Hist. (politely looking away): Are you sure that's what happened? Memory plays funny tricks. We hear other stories, you know. Think, now.

I did as he said. I thought for a moment or two, smelling my vomit, and I was still sure. I saw what I saw. I heard what I heard. I told him so stonily. I also had my own questions. Where had he heard other stories? From whom? I knew he was up to something.

Hist. (evasively): I appreciate the strain you're under, know that, but it seems to me with everything that was going on the other day, as you describe it, you couldn't possibly recall—

I interrupted him. I did not like the implications of his remark. I did not like the tone, either; I do not take easily to condescension. I was beginning to despise him for that; in my view, it was unworthy of a historian. Already, only an hour into our exchange, I was beginning to recognize in myself a perverse urge to mislead him, was developing a powerful desire to lie—a need, in fact. If he wanted a history that he could call his own, which would enhance the self-esteem of the Yankee Division, I'd give him one. But I told him the truth again, for the third time. "And," I added politely, "I am not going to tell this story again. Sir." I underlined the "Sir" and made him blush. He was a captain as well as a historian, and captains do not like to be rebuked by privates first class.

My questioner grew somber. He stroked his furry Brit-style mustache with his thumb, smoothing it out on either side of his upper lip, taking his time. Certainly it was his prerogative. Together we had all the time in the world. Then, finished with his mustache, he lit a cigarette, without offering me one.

I could tell that the captain was one of those lonely officers who were without a command. I had seen the type before. No one reported to him; no one ever would. He didn't give orders; he had no one to give orders to. All he had was a dubious authority, derived from his professional specialty. Somehow I felt that he didn't have any buddies, either. The spinster type—Mr. Go-It-Alone, intellectually superior. Here at the base hospital, sitting across from me, wetting his thumb to smooth out his mustache again, he looked as though he might be getting ready to cry. I would have liked to see that, the captain crying from a frustration that I had created. His poor history. The poor story he wanted me to tell that would heighten the self-importance of the Yankee Division, the one he knew before he even met me. And then the real one, the one I was trying to tell him, which he had been forced to listen to so many times today. It had to be bitter for him.

"I better clean this mess up," I said, looking down at my vomit.

"I think that might be wise," he said, and got up to go.


WE WERE finished for the day. We had had enough of each other. I could feel his relief. Besides, it was time for lunch. At noon, at all mealtimes, I soon discovered, the base came to frantic life, as though each meal might be the last. There was a sense of liberation everywhere, a welcome sociability among the hospital personnel, which I would have liked to share. But I was only an ambulatory patient there. I would soon be on my way to somewhere else. And it was their institution, in which I was just among the first of many interchangeable parts to have arrived. I had to keep reminding myself of that.

Overhead, at the moment, Lonesome Charlie was buzzing us from a rather low altitude. He was always there, every day in good weather, I would learn, observing us from a rickety enemy plane that was trying to keep an eye on what was going on behind the Third Army's lines. The plane was unarmed, I'm sure, and probably carried only a camera besides Charlie himself. Everybody kidded about Lonesome Charlie and pretended to pay no attention to him, as though they all, doctors and nurses alike, were truly without fear. But everybody, I noticed, always had one eye cocked to the sky when he was overhead. No point, I guess, in being overconfident.

After lunch, it was the psychiatrist's turn. (They were going to keep me busy, whatever the cost.) The good doctor was another captain without a command. He, too, never gave an order. He was also somber-looking and round-shouldered (perhaps from the weight of the stories that his patients had loaded on him), with thick eyebrows that dominated his face. At the top of his long, thin nose he wore granny specs; and for some reason he made me think of Ira Fedderman. While he was as interested in my narrative as his colleague, he was also just as interested in me. This softened me up, of course. I liked the chance to talk about myself. Answering lots of personal questions about my past life, such as it was, about my personal interests, my failed education, about books I had read, music, playing the piano (but not sex; we never got to that). He was deft at it, too, within his limitations, drawing me out without too much pain so that I talked a lot, probably too much, dramatizing myself, trying to make myself look good—as always.

What was needed first of all, he explained to me, was a diagnosis of my case. Only then could he do his medical duty and decide how to treat me. "You understand that?" he asked.

"I think so," I said.

But I began to wonder. For the first time, I was being asked to think of myself as a case, rather than as a patient. It seemed to me that there was a crucial difference there, one that I could not quite define but that brought me up sharply as the doctor continued to explain the process we would share. I listened carefully. The gist of it, he explained, was that together we would descend into the stony trenches of memory, in search of the recalcitrant past—his image— while supporting each other in perfect mutual trust.

I supposed so, even though the image sounded stale to me, as though it had been over-rehearsed.


PSYCH.: Son.

Me: Sir?

Psych.: No need for formalities. It's doctor-patient here.

Me: Yes, sir.

Psych.: Anyway . . . Please try to describe your feelings again. Don't be shy about it. I assure you you have my total confidence. This time just try to be a little more specific, try not to use abstract words, like "fine" and "all right." You understand that, don't you? It'll make things easier. And faster. You'll see. Does that sound okay with you?

Did he really need my agreement? I doubted it. It was probably just his way of talking, a technique. All doctors have one. It's like a suit of armor for the medical profession. Technique. I tried to describe my feelings to him, always looking for a specific word. It was hard. I was not used to describing my feelings, or even thinking about them. As I've said, they gave me the hives. I wandered then, lost in the sticky maze of emotions. The good doctor did not seem to be surprised. He cleared his throat as I stumbled along, and slumped forward toward me. His granny specs slipped down his nose. I could feel his sympathy and his hunger for information. So I tried to make him happy by telling him again what had happened. That seemed the most direct way to my emotions, even though the sound of my own voice, its all-too-familiar pitch and timbre, like the whine of an oboe or some other reedy instrument, was beginning to get on my nerves. I began to talk about the squad, that's what it always seemed to come down to: about Ira Fedderman especially, about Johnson and his arm wound, about Paul Willis and Barney Barnato, about Rocky and Brewster and Natale. Then I talked about Bern. I grew excited. I wept.

Psych. (in an even tone): Rest a minute, son. Don't push yourself. We've probably done enough for one day. (He checked his watch.) You're doing fine. Just relax. Try to breathe a little less strenuously. Try not to waste your energy.

He put a hand on my shoulder as I continued to weep. With his palm resting there lightly, I could feel him thinking. There were actual vibrations, of the most tremulous delicacy, passing from the flat of his hand onto the skinny knobs of my shoulder. He was shuffling diagnoses, perhaps, as though they were playing-cards. He was considering alternatives while he quivered with thoughtfulness. Had I suffered shell shock? Combat fatigue? Was I malingering? Even through my excitement, I understood that he

was making a judgment, as well as a diagnosis, seeking a
name for my case that would explain everything and provide a defining tag for me, one that would shape my future
and mark the way I would think about myself for the rest
of my life. I understood that clearly and realized its impor-
tance. I told myself that I must try to appear less agitated.
I must seem to be in control of myself. Not skewed, not
crazy. I knew that "crazy" would suit the doctors only too
well. I sat up straight, looked attentive. I tried to brighten,
to actually cast a glow, while the doctor continued to think
about me with a sad expression on his face, his hand in
place on my shoulder. I could still feel the vibrations, but
fainter now. I had to make him like me. It seemed urgent.
In a moment, ever alert, ever cunning, I smiled.

WHAT would his report say? I tried to imagine it:
    Psych.: Soldier is nineteen. Five foot eight, 144 pounds.
Sandy crew-cut. Blue-eyed. High sensibility. High suscepti-
bility. Suffers chronic eczema, hives, muscle cramps, horni-
ness, and other ailments common to adolescence. Perhaps
emotionally immature—somewhat. Sole unwounded survivor of engagement at or near Bézange-la-petite. (I knew the
name because the historian had told me, spelling it out
carefully. Sometimes it's called Moncourt Woods.) Normal
guilt feelings at survival, combined with powerful frustrated
aggression resulting from twelve-hour siege, during which
soldier did not fire a single round of ammunition at the
enemy. Etc. Etc. Etc.
    Well, why not? It was a start, I thought, but only a start,
nowhere near enough. What about childish shame at pas-
sive behavior? That should be first in any report. Or terror

at the idea of returning to the front? There was that, too—
excessively. Or even the heavy grit of bitterness, which was
beginning to settle inside me like a layer of soot that would
never be removed, never erased, down to the last abrasive
black particle? That was there, too, along with everything
else just beginning to take hold.

Actually, I wanted to speak to my new friend from the
warmth of my heart, from its familiar heat, but I felt as
though I was freezing to death.


IN A moment, the doctor began again. I had my breathing
under control. I had myself under control. I was still smiling, intermittently—but smiling.

Psych.: Tell me about your family.

Me: What does my family have to do with it?

Psych.: Our families have to do with everything.

Me: Well, they don't have anything to do with this. (My
smile vanished.)

Psych.: I'm not pushing you. Just think about it a little.

Me: I don't want to talk about my family. They're three
thousand miles away. (The thought of my family, ignorant
of my state, three thousand miles away, brought tears to
my eyes; my newly found poise was ruined.) I don't want
them to know anything about this, either—I mean that.
Nobody's going to write home to them, are they?

Psych.: Not a word. Not from me. (He held up both
hands, palms out.) Heaven forbid. Where are you from,
anyway?

Me: Baltimore.

Psych.: I was in Baltimore once.

Me: I don't want anybody to write to my family.

Psych.: Trust me. You have my word. Now tell me, son
(a pause while he searched for what he wanted to say), tell
me, you love music, so do I. Let's talk a bit about music.
Who is your favorite composer?

My favorite composer? Now I had to think up answers
to silly cultural questions. But maybe it was really what I
wanted to talk about. I mean, it seemed innocent. Still, I
had to ask myself, was there a correct answer here, for
which I would get a perfect mark, an A? And, by extension,
enhance my record with the good doctor? If there was, I
had to find it. I wanted the doctor's approval.

Psych.: Anyone in particular? Beethoven, say? He's
always good to start with.

Me: Oh sure. Beethoven.

Psych.: Do you play the sonatas?

Me: One or two of the early ones. Sort of. You know
what I mean.

Psych. (nodding): And Bach?

Me: Oh sure, Bach, too. Certainly. Ira Fedderman liked
Berlioz. Berlioz was his favorite. He wanted me to like
him, too. He used to call him Hectoring Berlioz. He liked
him a lot.

Psych.: I can believe that. I like him, too. Hectoring
Berlioz, that's pretty good. I can see the point.

Me: Yes.

Psych.: Well, we all have our favorites. I guess you could
do worse.

And I have others, I wanted to say. A dozen more. They
change from day to day. My tastes are fickle. It's one of my
worst faults. Just ask my friends.

But the doctor apparently had the answers he was looking for. At least, he didn't ask anything more about com-

posers. Did that mean that Beethoven and Bach sufficed? Perhaps they would help to absolve me. A lot was at stake. My life, perhaps. The doctor then made a suggestion, proceeding with care.

Psych.: Son, I don't want you to misunderstand what I'm going to say now.

Me: No, sir.

Psych.: It's important for you to know that we have your well-being at heart and that we have ways to help you feel better. Tested ways. Safe. But I don't want to put you in a position where you'll be doing anything against your will.

He paused. We looked at each other. It was too abstract for me. He had to be more specific. Watching him, I had the sudden feeling that he was actually very shy, that this interview was painful for him, too. This brought on a rush of sympathy in me. I wanted the doctor to feel comfortable. How could I assure this? I waited for him to go on. I was thinking about what he had said about doing something against my "will." Nobody in the Army had ever talked about that before.

Psych. (pleasantly): Did you hear what I just said?

I nodded and smiled a ghastly smile.

Psych.: There are new techniques. The latest in medical advances. We have full access, even here at the front.

What front? I didn't see any front. Everybody at the base hospital, I was discovering, liked to talk like that, as though they were risking their lives every day, as though they were in actual combat. The real front was miles away. Miles. Although you could still hear the big guns and their echoing aftermath from time to time. I remained silent. Orderlies and doctors and a few nurses hovered nearby, talking shop. The women's voices were among the first I had heard in many weeks; they were full of wisecracks and promise. But I was getting impatient. I began to squirm. I wanted this confrontation to be over. The doctor and I were sitting in a corner of a tent, facing each other on metal barrels. Our feet dangled uncomfortably in the air. The doctor spoke quietly to enhance the illusion of privacy. It almost worked. He glanced at my thumb every now and then while we sat there. So did I. It was still bandaged and the bandage was filthy. I tried to hide it.

I waited for him to go on.

"For example," he said, "we have a serum available to us that will relax you, help you to sleep, even help you to talk."

"Hmm," I said.

"I recommend it," he answered. "It's very effective."

"Ira Fedderman," I said, "went to a psychiatrist once in Brooklyn. The principal of his high school made him. He wouldn't let him back in school unless he went. Ira Fedderman told me about it. He told me that—"

"Ira Fedderman is not the subject here, son," the doctor said, suddenly frosty. "Let's try to remember that."

"Do you think I'm having trouble talking?" I asked, returning to the subject.

He hesitated a moment, considering. He pushed at his specs. I liked his specs; they were flattering. They took attention away from his eyebrows and his long, thin nose. I wanted them for myself. I thought they would look good on me. Better than on him. "Well," he said, "what I'm talking about operates like a truth serum. You know? You've heard of that, haven't you?" He faked a laugh.

"You mean the stuff really makes you tell the truth?" I asked. I was perfectly straight-faced.

"Right. It helps you to relive your experiences and then helps you to talk about them. Of course, I'm simplifying."

"What kind of experiences?"

"Well, painful ones, mainly. Those you have trouble surfacing. Those you choose to block. Like the one you just went through."

I changed my mind about his shyness then. I began to think that he was merely clumsy and, what's more, didn't care; and further, that part of the clumsiness may have come from the fact that I was his first patient. Literally. It was as though he had just opened his first office, which happened to be located in the wilds of Alsace-Lorraine, and I wandered in unexpectedly. More patients, of course, could be expected to arrive at any moment.

"I don't have any trouble talking about what happened to me," I said. "I've been talking to you for hours."

"Look, it's for seismic events," he said. "The big ones, the ones we have trouble assimilating. The serum actually acts like a kind of soul balm," he went on, "if you want a poetic description." Here he laughed in self-deprecation. "I have to try it, you know. I really do. With your cooperation, of course."

"You *have* to?" I asked. I was pitiless.

"Yes, I'm obligated in my role as division psychiatrist. I must use everything that is available to me on behalf of my patients. But I want you to understand that I firmly believe in these techniques. They're the wave of the future. I have faith. They promise great rewards."

There I was sitting on this metal barrel in a corner of the tent with all the medical buzz going on around me, all the benign, health-giving chatter, and it was all somewhat confusing. It was making me tired, and I was shaking again. I could see the shaking and so could the doctor. It was impossible to hide, especially my hands, and I was still having intermittent weeping fits, which mortified me. I couldn't help them, I didn't even want to, so I said to myself, Screw it, go for some of the great rewards the doctor just mentioned, what can you lose?

The answer, obviously, was my autonomy, fractured as it already was. Peculiar as it may sound, that didn't occur to me until I was already going under, the next morning, soon after the needle had delivered its first benevolent dose of the doctor's so-called soul balm into the veins of my upper left arm. Sodium pentothal, the doctor called it, when I asked him. He could hardly wait.

I CERTAINLY talked. The doctor was right about that. A floodstream of obsessive language was released. On and on, words rolling to infinity. It was the same old story, perhaps, but this time, for once, I was not interrupted. This time, too, my voice carried a greater authority, a real authority, that of the serum itself. Every word I spoke now could be believed by the doctor; the integrity of his science assured it.

I lay prone on a canvas cot in the corner of another tent and talked to the doctor, who sat alongside me on a stool, notebook and pen in hand. A black Waterman, I remember, thick as a cigar. Every now and then as I talked, he would scribble something in his notebook—a word, phrase, a whole sentence perhaps—full of clues, I hoped, then lift his eyes and look down at me through his specs, nodding encouragingly. Not that I needed encouragement. The drug saw to that.

I think he was pleased. He certainly looked pleased, nodding at me like that. On the other hand, he would sometimes wince at a particularly graphic image, even though he had heard this story at least three times before, almost word for word—and I didn't try to make the images fresh, either; I didn't have that kind of control. What did it matter, anyway; it all sounded new to me in my present state, running off at the mouth while my voice shook. I was like a garrulous hostage trapped in an alien land, with an alien fluid running through my veins, bending my damaged mind to its whim. I talked, he listened. We had become the perfect couple, the doctor and I, meshed in passing.

Almost at the very end of my monologue, the doctor suddenly said, "By the way, what did you do to your thumb?"

I looked at it. "Cut it on a C ration can. I think."

"What do you mean you think?"

"I don't remember. I'm not sure."

He wrote something down. "Better get a clean bandage on that," he said after a moment. "No point in inviting infection. When did it happen?"

I couldn't remember. I couldn't even remember it happening.


THAT first session on sodium pentothal took about two hours, maybe less, and I fell into a deep sleep when it was over—the kind of sleep that is like a lost universe in itself, an entire vast dark underworld that leaves no trace of itself behind. Later—three, four hours later—I began my monologue again after I awoke, but this time, I soon learned, I had other things on my mind, all of them cryptically disjointed.

The Psych. was back in place, along with his notebook and Waterman, and another doctor, one I had never seen before, had joined him. We were introduced.

"Dr. X," the Psych. said. With a strange doctor present, his tone was suddenly crisper, as though he was afraid of being caught with an emotion. "He's one of our surgeons," he went on. "He has nothing to do with your case. He's only going to observe. I hope you don't mind." He was certainly clipping his words.

No, I didn't mind and indicated so. In fact, after a moment's thought, I rather liked the idea of having an audience of two. Maybe they would serve as a check on each other. Maybe they would help to assure the other's reliability. But I didn't tell them that.

As I said, I now had other things on my mind. I was finished with Bézange-la-petite for the moment, with machine-gun sweeps, mortar shells, snipers, and all the rest. It was the noise, really, that I was finished with, or trying to be finished with, but the noise of Bézange lasted. It still lasts.

"I wish you had known Ira Fedderman," I heard myself say.

"I wish I had, too," my doctor said, without a pause.

"He was really smart. Brilliant, actually."

"You've made him seem very vivid."

"When did I ever say anything about Ira Fedderman to you?" I really couldn't remember.

"Here and there in our talks. Berlioz, remember? Therapy? In Brooklyn?"

"He could really be fucking awful when he wanted."

"I thought you liked him."

" 'Like' was not the issue. 'Pity' was. Oh, I could really be fucking mean to him."

"I'm sure you weren't the only one," the Psych. said, making a note. "You know that type often makes other people behave badly. Sometimes deliberately."

"A sad fucking sack."

"What's all this fucking talk all of a sudden?"

"I always talk like that."

"Not with me you don't."

"Sorry."

"Don't apologize. You're always apologizing."

"Am I? Maybe I like to accommodate people."

"Just go on with what you were saying."

"Right. Fedderman. A sad fucking sack."

"Why are you punishing yourself for your friend's death?"

I waited a moment before answering. "Is that what I'm doing?" I finally asked.

"Think about it for a minute."

I thought about it. "Who knows?" I said. "He's dead."

"They're all dead, aren't they? Why single one out?"

I began to squirm. He was speaking the icy truth. And he was pushing me. I was supposed to take this at my own speed. Maybe it was the presence of the other doctor that did it.

"Paul Willis was another one," I then said. "A mother-fucking thief."

The Psych. was concentrating hard. His colleague, the surgeon, sat there deadpan, observing.

"Who was Paul Willis?"

"He was in the squad. He was our scout. He was the one who stole our shitty underwear."

The Psych. was now writing very fast. So was the other doctor. Why, I don't know. But it made me puff out. I couldn't help it. I felt that I was like a hero in a struggle that I had to win. Me, a hero? And the Psych.? Was he just another prick? I wondered about that.

"Don't misunderstand me," I went on. "Paul Willis was no asshole dummy. He had a hell of a lot going for him. It was just that one thing. Stealing. He was a hell of a lot smarter than Barney Barnato, with those nose-drip quotes of his from philosophy."

"Sounds like quite a crew," the Psych. said, trying a smile.

"Who knows?" I said. "They're all fucking dead. You just said it yourself."

And I was off again, racing through the mournful litany of names from the first squad and the third platoon, the ones I knew, telling the stories, their own, mine, everyone's. I must have talked for an hour, while my eyes tried to close on me. Sometimes I heard myself shout, as though my emotions were trying to catch up with my narrative. My voice began to grow hoarse. My mouth dried up. I had lost the ability to salivate for the moment. Even so, I never got to Bern Keaton, never even brought his name up—I thought that was strange when I remembered it later—and never did manage to mention Francis Gallagher, either—Lieutenant top-class, fucking A-1. That seemed even stranger.

· · ·

WHEN I finished, I said, "Do I have to see Captain H"—
meaning the division's historian—"again?"

"He's gone back to Division Headquarters," the Psych.
told me. "Where the big brass are. Is that okay with you?"

I tried to smile. "Why not? I hope he's happy." But I
didn't care two cents. He had his history. "Did Gangplank
Paul ever make it overseas?" I then asked.

"Of course."

"You've actually seen him?"

"Well, I can't swear . . ."

"Then don't be so sure."

He laughed at that. The idea seemed to please him.

"You know," I said, "about Ira Fedderman . . ."

"You look pretty tired to me," the doctor said, getting up
to go. "Maybe it's enough for one day."

I could hear some fuss going on outside the tent.

"We're going to run a few physical tests," he said.

"For what?"

"General stuff. I want to check out your circulation. I
want to make sure you're getting enough oxygen in your
system."

I breathed in deeply and exhaled. "How's that?"

"I want to make sure the oxygen is getting to your brain."

For some reason that struck me as funny. Oxygen. In my
brain. My fucking brain. Jesus, they thought of everything.
"What's all that noise out there?"

"They're bringing some wounded in," the surgeon said,
his first words of the day. "And I'd better go."

By then I didn't know whether I was awake or asleep.
Had I said all this aloud or was I just talking to myself? In
fact, I still don't know, to this day, and nothing in my experience helps or reassures me. Outside the tent, to the

north, there were a couple of artillery blasts, big ones. While I was still carrying on, still murmuring, as though I wanted to fix the pitch of what I was saying in my inner ear for all time, one of the orderlies came in to give me a shot. "It'll put you to sleep," he said, taking out a swab. I just stuck out my arm as though I was welcoming him, and in the needle plunged, like so many before it. This time, the effect lasted fourteen hours and burned me out, scoured me, down to my toes.

Later, I learned that the oxygen was flowing very neatly into my brain, just as it should. My circulation was working. At least, that was out of the way—the physical part, I mean.

# NINE

# Duffel Bags

IN ANOTHER three days, I had arrived in the city of Nancy, where my Psych., in collaboration with some of his cohorts at the base hospital, had decided to ship me for a while. The move, he explained, was designed to offer me some daily chores for which I would have full responsibility and, in the process, give me a chance to return to myself. That was what I seemed to need, above all—to go full circle. Of course, I leapt at the chance that he was offering me to get away from the front, to heal—as I'm sure he knew I would—but I nevertheless tried hard to hide my excitement at the prospect in case he might change his mind. It wasn't altogether clear to me then, but it is now—I no longer trusted anyone.

The Psych., I finally decided, was probably doing his best. He had tried hard to deal with me, or so I had to assume; but I had the clear feeling when we said good-bye that he couldn't wait to get rid of me. For one thing, for a man who rarely smiled, he was smiling a lot as we shook hands.

"Thanks for everything," I said, as I climbed into the back of a truck that was going to make a mail pickup in the city and then deliver me to my new post.

"Take care of yourself," the doctor said, in a kindly voice. "You're not out of the woods yet. And don't be shy. If you feel that you need me, you know where I am." Then he smiled some more and backed away from the truck's exhaust, coughing from the acrid fumes. I wanted to pat him on the back, to soothe him and show him I cared, but instead I just sat there, smiling too.

Actually, I appreciated what he said, even while doubting his sincerity. But why should I have worried about his sincerity? The important thing was that he had said it. I guess the real truth was that we were both a little sick of each other. I was even sicker of myself, and knew it. But there was no time to consider all that at the moment. I would have to remind myself of it later, for we were suddenly off to Nancy, far enough behind the lines, the driver revving up without a word of warning and stepping on the gas full-strength. In a moment, the doctor had become a blur behind me, then a dot. Finally, I lost him entirely. He was gone.

There was another soldier sitting across from me in the truck, slumped over in his seat. I eyed him without staring. I was careful about that. I could tell that he couldn't bear to be stared at. His pack rested between his legs, his helmet lay on the bench alongside him. His mouth was turned down at both corners. I knew the expression. Defeat and depression, also to be read in his lackluster eyes. Not one of the gods, definitely. We nodded at each other.

"Any idea how long it takes to get to Nancy?" I finally asked, in a friendly way, settling down on my bench slats. Without the drugs and the truth serum, in the absence of my soul balm, my voice sounded a little strange to me. I had trouble making it go at the right speed.

He didn't answer at first, but after a moment he said, "Dunno." Very slow, very lazy, but shrugging expressively as he spoke the single word. Then he looked out of the back of the truck at the road behind us, to avoid my eye.

I decided to introduce myself, shouting over the truck's engine. He had to look at me then. I don't know whether he heard my name or not. I waited. "Charlie Beale," he called back, showing small, squared-off, yellowing teeth. I could see how tall he was sitting there, tall and skinny and pigeon-toed.

"You going to the depot?" I asked.

"Yes."

"Been there before?"

"First time."

"Me, too."

He nodded again. "What happened to you?" I asked. That was a mistake, I instantly realized. The question had come too fast and too soon. I should have waited a few days, maybe even more, before asking that.

Charlie Beale looked mildly disappointed in me. And of course he didn't answer.

"I lost my whole platoon," I heard myself say, again too quickly. I felt myself flush. I had embarrassed myself. Was I beginning to boast about my little adventure? And was I beginning to enjoy the boasting?

There was a silence again. We stared at each other for another moment, then looked away. I knew I had ruined the exchange by my eagerness. I had always been over-eager and had ruined a lot of possibilities that way at school, especially with girls, speaking up too quickly. I would have to watch myself. Nobody likes people who talk too much, especially when they're strangers.

We drove on. The truck careened, the driver blowing his horn and scattering pedestrian traffic in front of us. Later, there was a brief stop at a jammed crossroad while our driver waited his turn to proceed. I breathed in the chilled autumn air, lit up a cigarette, gazed at the rustic scenery: trees and a couple of blasted houses. There was a lot of traffic moving toward Nancy, mostly Army trucks. The drivers were all yelling at each other. I didn't like the noise. It made me shake, but in a way I could control. Still silent, Charlie Beale and I avoided each other's eyes. We rattled along, already ten miles from the front, I guessed, and with each mile my sense of well-being increased. I took a little nap and woke up a few minutes later in a suburb. We were passing a sign advertising Dubonnet. I didn't even know what Dubonnet was. But actually, I was beginning to feel pretty good.


RAY Landis and Willie Goodenough were waiting for us at the depot when we arrived. They stood side by side on the front steps, tall and short, like cartoon figures, with their hands in their pockets, ready to make a judgment. (So were we.) More strangers, I thought, then proceeded to identify myself as we jumped off the truck. I had to say my name three times before they got it right.

"Okay," Ray Landis said, "your name's perfect inside my head, I can hear it clear as a bell, but I can't promise that

I can always get it out that way. What is it, anyway?" he asked, looking at me a little suspiciously.

"Polish. And Jewish."

"Hmm," Ray Landis said, eyeing me up and down as though he was looking for sinister protuberances. Horns, say. Willie Goodenough, who was the short one, as light-boned and slight as a drummer boy, said nothing. But he looked me up and down, too, from where he stood next to Ray Landis. What did he see in me? I would have liked to know. I marked him as a sidekick, disdainfully, somebody who ran errands and did other favors for the boss, who, in this case, was named Ray Landis.

"And I'm Beale," my new friend said unexpectedly, into the silence. "Charlie. Protestant and English. Half-English, anyway."

That little speech took me by surprise, given Charlie Beale's initial reticence, but I have to say for Ray Landis that he laughed at it, although not spontaneously. He just let a beat go by while he thought about it, then let loose. He had a big laugh and a big chest, about three feet across, like a wrestler. His laugh boomed out, a little too loud for me. Then, without comment, Ray Landis and Willie Goodenough took us into the depot's outer room, showed us the straw pallet we were to share with them at night, which measured about ten feet by ten, showed us where to stash our stuff on shelves along the wall, how to work the defective stove without burning the place down, and where rations were kept—in a metal drum, with a lid on it and a couple of bricks on top of the lid to keep the rats out. I could tell, from the way his eyes bulged at the word, that Charlie Beale was not happy about rats. Neither was I.

When they finished with the preliminaries, Ray Landis and Willie Goodenough took us into the warehouse itself. This turned out to be a vast, dilapidated shed built on concrete floors that had cracked here and there like ice floes. To move around, we had to jump from one broken section to another. Overhead, there were old unpainted iron beams supporting glass ceilings that were filthy with soot, like a nineteenth-century train station. Duffel bags filled the huge space, piled high in stacks that reached halfway to the ceiling. The shed was probably the length of a football field. I stared at all the baggage, at the endless rows of green canvas bags. I had never seen so many duffels in one place.

Landis pointed out the rat droppings while Charlie's eyes bulged again. He also indicated where the most serious leaks in the ceiling were, warned us against smoking in the duffel bag area itself, and only then got down to business.

"We've been doing this single-handed," he said, pointing at Willie Goodenough and himself, "so you could say that we're glad to see you. Right, Will?" Will nodded. He came up to Ray's shoulder. "Anyway, you see all those duffel bags," Landis went on. "They're pretty hot stuff. Worth a lot of money and sentiment, but non-negotiable." Landis paused a moment to laugh at his own joke. Already it was clear that he had a philosophy about duffel bags, and I admired him for it. It gave him a kind of clarity. "There's a duffel bag in here for every frigging GI in the YD," he went on. "Think about that. And they're not just sitting around helter-skelter, every man for himself. It's all a careful system. If you know the system, and you will, you'll be able to find your own bag in five minutes. Less, even."

Our job, Ray Landis continued, was to guard the ware-house. That was part one, he explained, and pretty damn important. The warehouse, he added, was a prime target for black marketeers. He let that one sink in, looking serious. Willie did the same. I guess it was serious. I mean, black marketeers. I had never known a black marketeer, but where I came from they had a rotten reputation.

The second part of the job, Landis said, was also pretty damn important. It was to pick out the duffel bags of YD casualties, mostly the dead. Again, Charlie Beale's eyes began to work when Landis explained this. Mine probably did, too. It was a little hard to take in. After the bags had been separated out, Landis went on, as though he was offering us a bonus, we would then open and ransack them for personal effects, which would eventually be gathered together and shipped home to the next of kin in the USA. A going-away, never-to-return present, I thought, feeling myself heading into a stupor—a morbid cottage industry guaranteed to grow to factory size, and soon.

This was to be my treatment, as developed at the base hospital by the good doctor. It would be Charlie Beale's as well, whatever he was suffering from. (Plenty, it seemed obvious to me, from the way he looked.) This would be how we would recuperate and find our beloved selves again, by keeping an eye out for black marketeers and thieves, and by plundering the dead behind their backs.

After Ray Landis had finished his explanations, we began to wander back to our "quarters." Willie Good-enough had disappeared, without explanation—not that he owed us any. The shed smelled of stale water and guano. I looked up past the iron beams to see if there were any signs of bat nests around. (Bats vaguely bothered me, too.) Charlie looked depressed again, as though he had taken in all he could for one day. I felt pretty much like that myself. Stuporous, as I've said. I had heard enough for the moment. But Ray Landis had more to say.

"No officers around, either," he began, rolling his eyes. "Not bad, as long as we keep our noses clean, don't make trouble, make sure the duffel bag count is up-to-date. That's the point of the whole thing, the count. If you ask me, we're pretty damn lucky to be here, when you consider." (Much nodding from Charlie Beale at this.) "Hot food gets delivered once in a while, mail every three days. We make our own duty roster, share and share alike. It's important for all of us to get out every now and then—not at the same time, of course. It's not a bad town. If you like frogs. Whores all over the place. If you like that kind of thing."

He rolled his eyes again, lubriciously, and gave a small ambiguous smile, suggesting perhaps that liking such a thing was probably an impossibility for Charlie and me. Charlie smiled back, showing his yellow teeth. I didn't respond. I never did in such conversations. I had too much to hide. The secret of my life was that I was still a virgin, and I intended to keep the secret my own. I didn't know about Charlie Beale. Or Ray Landis. For that matter, I wasn't sure about anybody in the Yankee Division.

"So," Ray Landis wound up, suddenly sounding domestic, "make yourself at home. I'll get some coffee going. Be sure the lid is always on top of the stove or we'll burn like Joan of Arc." He paused here to give us a piercing look. "Another thing," he said, "we have a bath every other day. That's a rule and regulation. There's a tub just outside the door. I think it was used for dyeing stuff in the olden days, and we collect rainwater for the purpose. Go easy on the water. There's always enough, so far, but still no reason to be profligate."

As I would soon learn, Ray Landis liked three-syllable words. They represented a simple challenge for him, and Ray liked challenges, especially if they could be met. But, for all that, he was surprisingly ignorant of the great world around him. It was as though his experience did not quite match his curiosity, so that he was always having to play catch-up. He claimed, for example, when we knew each other better, that I was his first "Joo." Where he came from, in Utah, there were no "Jooz." I believed that. And I believed that his curiosity was innocent, that his questions totally lacked malicious intent.

Why do Jooz always live in cities? he wanted to know. I thought that was a legitimate question. Why do they always live together? Why do they look down on the gentiles? (No offense, he quickly added.) How had they lasted so long? Why *were* they?

Patiently, I explained what I understood of the matter. (It is true that when a Jew is faced with such questions, he feels responsible for the safety and well-being of every other Jew. Each word must carry its real weight, each answer fit the case. In short, an accurate response must be made; it is the heart of the matter.) I related history, anecdotes, horror stories of the past. I described pogroms, persecution, treachery. And I have to say for Ray Landis that he paid attention.

I'll have to think about all that, he said when I finished. There's plenty there to cogitate about. Hmm, he began, trying to assimilate the exchange. Willie Goodenough was listening, too, but silently. God knows what he was thinking. You could never tell with Willie. Charlie Beale, meanwhile, stood behind him, tall and skinny, warming himself at the stove and looking quizzical at Ray's responses. I was growing to like Charlie. There was a sweet modesty about him, an unresisting diffidence that made me want to draw him out, sure that I would hear something unexpected, maybe even memorable. Early on, Charlie had nicknamed Willie Goodenough "Boris." I thought that was pretty unexpected, and I really appreciated it. Charlie had his wits about him. He was smart, but with no edge. I liked that. But Charlie still hadn't told me what had happened to him—had never, in fact, referred to it.

"And what brought *you* here?" I finally asked Ray Landis, when we had finished with the Jews. I thought that was a simple enough challenge, and I tried to make it sound as though I was talking about the weather.

"None of your frigging business," he answered, smiling at my nerve.


WE BEGAN to thread our lives together, in the most ordinary way. Housekeeping routines were established, schedules organized. In-ter-de-pen-den-cy, Ray called it— a jackpot word. And it worked, with a minimum of shoving and pulling. It worked because each of us insisted on it. It was a matter of mutual pride and necessity. Nobody ever raised a voice in that echoing shed, nobody made absurd demands, or demands of any kind. (Our bad tempers and natural irritability we each kept for ourselves, alone.) And we were careful never to crowd each other—never, if possible, to touch. Only at night, when one of us might roll over on the vast straw pallet we shared, was there ever a problem, solved in an instant with a simple apology.

We took alternate shifts, Ray and Willie Goodenough, Charlie and I. While they guarded the warehouse, we began to wander around town, tentatively at first, a little gun-shy. We were both uneasy and still shaky out in this new urban world we were exploring, almost as though we were learning how to walk again. Anything might set us off. A strange street noise on our travels, an artillery-like discharge from an Army truck, could trigger a fast retreat to the warehouse, and no questions asked. But in each other's near-silent presence we could pretend to be almost normal, and we soon found enough confidence to make it all the way to the Place Stanislas, where we admired the rococo iron grillwork and the impressive statuary that filled the square. Charlie seemed to know a lot about that kind of thing. We even settled on a favorite café on the square—favorite because the waiter recognized us the second time we showed up, boosting our confidence—and learned to sip cognac in the middle of the day without losing our equilibrium. Charlie was better at it than I: two cognacs to my one, as though his were milk.

The Place Stanislas was the heart of the city; everything in Nancy began and ended there, and the sight of French civilian street life suddenly revealed in all its common-placeness, gave us a shock. We wondered about all these vigorous Gauls, bustling about in their strange civvie clothes, confidently ignoring us. The women in their wedgies and swept-up hair, the men in their stiff wartime suits, rigid as boards. Did they know what was going on just a few miles north of their beautiful little city? Did they have

sense enough to feel threatened? And did they know what
had happened to me, and, by extension, to Charlie?
Prickly questions, never asked aloud by either of us, as isolated strangers making our way through town.

Sometimes, for these excursions, Charlie and I would
trade partners, and I would find myself walking the streets
of Nancy with Ray Landis. Ray talked a lot as we wandered around the city—talking was one of the things he
was good at—mostly about whores, and whorehouses, and
the sexual proclivities (his word, of course) of French
women. Ray had quite a range. The strength of a French
vagina, for example; the French addiction to oral sex; the
French eagerness to experiment; and other matters of equal
sophistication. I questioned nothing. What did I know? I
believed everything I was told. But Ray never, to my knowledge, made an actual move of his own in that direction. It
was all talk, obsessively driven. He finally confessed to me
that he had been raised as a Mormon, as though that
explained everything. Perhaps it did.

As Ray had said, our situation was not bad, as long as we
kept our noses clean. The hot food arrived, as promised,
every now and then—stew, it was called. Mail, too, poured
in, the first since Normandy, fourteen letters in one deliv-
ery for me alone, a dozen of them from my mother, who
wrote as though America existed on another planet, in
another orbit, in a perpetual springtime. But what a feast
for me, reading and re-reading those letters.

Our stove, meanwhile, remained a constant threat. All
four of us slept with one eye open as the sparks flew
throughout the night. But no real damage was done—one
singed sock belonging to Charlie and a burn on Private
Goodenough's thumb, which was his fault. And not a sin-

gle black marketeer ever showed up; nobody ever tried to corrupt us.

This peculiar domesticated life went on for several weeks. We got on together, knowing what was needed. I answered all of Ray Landis's questions about the Jews, and he responded to mine about the Mormons, delicately explaining the history and significance of polygamy, which was what really interested me, and trying hard to clarify the usual misconceptions about his religion. (If it actually was still his religion; I suspected that he was a serious backslider and was still too unsure of himself to talk about it to an outsider.) I finally learned, too, that Charlie Beale was an engineer, out of the artillery; that he was also, once you got beyond his modesty, a kind of expert on baroque music, of which there were very few in 1944; and that he played the organ, sometimes in public recitals, in Dayton, Ohio, his hometown—all news that amazed me. Of Goodenough, I learned little. He was from Philly, as he called it, he pasted up billboard signs for a living, and he had never finished high school. There the information stopped.

We had made an infinitely tiny world of our own, held together by personal consideration and mutual responsibility, which we never failed to honor. That seemed to me a real achievement, given the universe that tiny world was a part of. All we hoped for was that we would be forgotten by the military machine, that the war would pass us by, that we would be left forever in the city of Nancy to guard the duffel bags of the Yankee Division. These shared hopes had caused us to grow cozy together, a folly in wartime. I had learned that lesson several times before.

When a jeep pulled up in front of the depot one morning and an imperious young corporal leapt out and asked for Private Goodenough, we lost our innocence and our sidekick, all at once. He was gone within a half-hour, back to his unit. Poor Willie, packed into the rear seat of the jeep, refusing to look at us as the jeep pulled away.

"I'm next," Ray Landis said mournfully, watching his pal go. "It's a sure thing."

I didn't contradict him. It *was* a sure thing that one of us would be next. Which one? Without a word, then, Charlie nervously began to do his laundry for a second time that week, and I decided to take a walk on my own, to worry about the question alone.

The next day, another jeep pulled up, this time bringing Willie's replacement, a vast swarthy giant, with bones like a dinosaur's, whose name I can no longer remember (something Slavic, I think, something Rumanian). But it was too late for this stranger. We didn't have it for him. The energy for a new friendship, or even a companionable collaboration, had been dissipated in the effort we had all made for each other. We were exhausted by it. And Willie Goodenough's melancholy departure had proved again, in case we had forgotten, just how vulnerable we were. No, the ties were coming loose, that much was clear; events were beginning to take over again, and we were starting to grow uneasy.

THEN, what had to happen finally happened. Orders came through to separate out the duffel bags of the third platoon, C Company, 104th regiment. It was the obvious possibility to which I had blinded myself for weeks while I was sipping cognac in the Place Stanislas in the middle of the day and listening to Charlie Beale talk about baroque composers I had never heard of. How could I have been surprised?

It was a job I had to do—there was no other way—and of course I chose Charlie to do it with me. We began right after breakfast. I didn't want to waste time. I wanted the job behind me. We moved fast at first, stumbling over ourselves. The "system" Ray Landis had talked about was that within each unit all the bags were stacked in very rough alphabetical order. As stupidly simple as that.

I was demanding with Charlie, even querulous, as though I was some kind of superior NCO who ruled the roost. As though I owned everything. But I soon settled down, in the face of the reproving look Charlie gave me. He was standing at the top of the pile, calling off the names that were stenciled on each of the bags, before tossing them down to me on the floor below.

So we proceeded, through half a dozen vaguely familiar names, echoes of the second and third squads, remnants of old roll calls. Peters. Schwartz. Juneman. Oliver. Reese. Schiffman. Green. Each time Charlie called a name, he threw a bag to me, and I tried to catch it—all that was left of those who were killed or missing in action at Bézange-la-petite.

"P. Willis," Charlie called after resting a moment.

I paused. "Here!" I yelled.

Then "Roger Johnson." There was an echo in the shed, Charlie's voice bouncing back at us. I looked up at the filthy glass ceiling, checking for bats.

"Yo!" I shouted. The bag fell like a corpse alongside me.

"Barnett Barnato." Charlie was beginning to acquire a kind of rhythm that carried us along.

"Barnett?"

"Barnett Barnato," Charlie repeated, pronouncing Barney's mysterious surname on the first instead of the second syllable. "*Bar*-na-toe," when it was really "Bar-*nah*-toe." For some reason, this irritated me. It seemed important, the correct pronunciation of everybody's name; even Barney's.

"*Ja!*" I finally yelled. I piled his bag on top of Johnson's.

"There's rat shit up here," Charlie said. I could hear a shudder in his voice. "R. Hubbell," he called, after a moment.

R. Hubbell, I thought. Capers and beautitudes. "Toss it," I called up.

The work was getting warm. Charlie and I were both in a sweat. "Want to break for a couple of minutes?" I asked. I was beginning to smell myself, and Charlie, I saw when I looked up, was sniffing shyly at his armpits.

"Let's keep going while we have some momentum," Charlie said. That was all right with me. Then, "I. Fedderman."

I waited a moment.

"I. Fedderman," Charlie said again.

What was I waiting for?

"Fedderman!" This time Charlie was shouting.

"*Ici!*" I shouted back and felt Fedderman's bag hit me on the shoulder. It hurt. It was filled with jagged edges, boxlike objects, unidentifiable sticks or rods, things that were sharp and strange. What did he have in there, for God's sake? My shoulder began to ache from the onslaught. I found myself cursing Ira Fedderman. Again. It never seemed to end. What in the hell could his personal effects amount to? What had he collected and stashed in his duffel bag over the many months since we began basic training at Fort Benning? Why hadn't I written to his mother? When would I?

At last Charlie was growing impatient. I couldn't blame him. He was tired of searching out duffel bags that belonged to men he didn't know or had never heard of, and he was weary of tossing them around. They weighed a lot. He began to complain.

I interrupted him. "Is there a Keaton up there?"

A minute passed. "I don't see one," Charlie called. But I didn't think he was trying very hard.

"Look carefully."

It took him a while but he finally found it. "Yours is here, too," he said. "And somebody Brewster. Want them?"

"Forget mine. Just toss the others down."

The bags landed at my feet. I had almost the whole squad now. "Any Natale?" I asked. I had to spell the name for Charlie.

"Nothing," he finally said.

No duffel bag for Ralph Natale. No personal effects. Was that possible? It made me feel strange, as though I had failed him, as though he was being cheated for a second time. Charlie was moving around on top of the pile again. He sounded restless. I could hear the soft thud as he jumped from one duffel bag to another. "Just one more," I said.

"Who?"

"Gallagher, Lieutenant."

Charlie began rummaging around and muttering to himself. "There aren't any officers up here that I can see," he said.

"You sure?" I asked.

I waited for him to check it out again. The smell of guano mixed with my own acrid sweat was beginning to get to me. It was a stink.

"They must be in a special section," Charlie said.

I waved him off. I was too tired and a little sick to my stomach. "Let's break," I said. We had done everything we could do. Dozens of duffel bags littered the floor around me, as evidence. Someone else would have to do the ransacking. Not me. Not me, for sure.

I thought I heard a scurrying sound then, coming from a corner of the shed. It was the click of rats' feet. It was a sound that I sometimes heard at night, while the four of us lay sprawled on our straw pallet. It always made me shudder. Willie Goodenough had claimed that the rats liked to gnaw their way through our duffel bags in search of food. Candy. Whiskey. Cigarettes. Even soap. They ate anything. Paul Willis's bag, in fact, had holes in it, jagged bites, all up and down one side. While I listened, I held on to Bern's duffel bag. I knew everything he had in there. Books. Extra fatigues. Tobacco. One blanket. A religious object or two. I had seen him pack it in the States, item by item, back at Camp Jackson, just before we headed overseas. It suddenly felt very heavy. I put it down and sat on it and watched Charlie slide down from the top of the pile. He had two huge sweat marks under his arms. I think I remembered to thank him. I hope I did, but I can't be sure. I was at absolute zero. There seemed to be nothing left except the sharp hallucinatory clicking of rats' feet and the sound of Charlie Beale's heavy breathing as he lighted a cigarette, against Ray Landis's strict warnings. I hated those foraging rats. They scared me. They gave me the *Schreck*. They gave Charlie Beale the *Schreck*, too. They made him crazy.

I had to get out of there.

# TEN

# No Trumpets, No Drums

I WAS transferred a few weeks later, through the collaboration of the division's Psych., from the warehouse in Nancy to an intelligence outfit that did research on captured enemy weapons. Maybe I should have been there all along, helping the outfit do its work; it seemed to suit me. I found the research interesting, serious, too, and remote from the infantry, as everything that is not the infantry is remote from it. And that was what I needed—some distance that could not be easily violated. I was grateful for the move. In a sense, you could say that my real war stopped on a shattered rise in the Moncourt Woods, at Bézange. The rest of the war, for me, was mere footnotes and asides—important, perhaps, but still a subtext made up of subsidiary themes.

I never saw Charlie Beale or Ray Landis again, and never heard from them, nor they from me. Something ended in that blighted warehouse in Nancy; something was concluded, once and for all.

. . .

THE REST of the story, the Yankee Division's story, was far from finished. There was more to come—there always is in wartime—a continuing zigzag journey, an often bitter march through the heart of Europe that carried the veteran division to the Ardennes, and the Battle of the Bulge and on into Germany and ultimately Czechoslovakia, at the war's end, when the 26th came face-to-face with the Russians outside the town of Budweis. The next day, they both officially met in the middle of the town square and enthusiastically shook hands, grinning mightily as though they had just accidentally run into each other—then did it all over again, still grinning, for the news cameras.

There had been major engagements everywhere, in France and Germany and the Ardennes during the Bulge, small skirmishes as well, ambushes, tank traps, passing firefights, full-scale onslaughts that involved the whole division . . . and many casualties. In the 104th alone, 666 men died and 2,575 were wounded; 35 remained missing in action. And once again, as in World War I, the 104th was awarded the Croix de Guerre by the French, alone among the YD regiments.

The official Yankee Division history, for which I was a presumed source, barely mentions Bézange-la-petite, glossing over the episode in a way that makes it impossible to discover what actually happened or whether, in fact, anything happened at all. It's both empty and evasive. (I wonder if the division's historian considered that a "victory"—over me, that is.) Of course, the careless loss of almost an entire platoon—and more—is not necessarily what divisional histories are designed to commemorate.

The inflated smell of distant glory is more their style. So I had learned back at the base hospital, and so, I think, I had always known. All of us had, probably to the last man.

The same is true of the official *U.S. Army History of World War II*. The volume called *The Lorraine Campaign*, in the course of nearly seven hundred densely packed pages, never refers to C Company's catastrophic loss at Bézange, even though there are at least a half-dozen listings of Bézange in the volume's index. Heavily detailed with numbers, citations, maps, and dates, *The Lorraine Campaign*, while keeping the chronology and statistics in order, nevertheless manages to give the impression that the war in Alsace-Lorraine was fought by an agglomeration of trucks, half-tracks, tanks, and humanoids in uniform, who may have resembled real men, in a physical sense, but who pretty much went through the motions of fighting without having to carry the burden of either names or authentic faces.

The 104th regimental history does it better. Maybe it's a simple matter of scale or of being closer to the subject or even of a more manageable ambition. The 104th's own history is far more specific and at times even slightly romantic in tone. Its restrained narrative names names and places, calls a disaster a disaster, and is enriched here and there by curiously lyrical interludes, especially when the facts cannot effectively carry the narrative.

In its restraint, the history catches something essential about the real experience, even while it avoids the central question for the handful of us who survived: that of accountability. Who actually was responsible for that day at the Horseshoe? C Company's commander? Battalion's? And what did it ultimately cost him, or them? (I would dearly like to know, but I have accepted the fact that it will probably remain unfinished business, safely buried, in the Army's terms, forever.) But the 104th's history, in general, doesn't avoid bad news. It is easy while reading its pages to recognize the voice of a thoughtful writer—or group of writers, since these narrative efforts were almost always collaborative—when it concludes, in a reflective passage about Bézange that "compared to the activities of the Western Front as a whole, these actions were insignificant—a minor engagement on a nameless [*sic*] hill somewhere in France. Yet to the regiment, they, as the initial combat encounters, were all-important. With them came the first shock of battle, the realization that combat means closing with the enemy and that closing with the enemy meant, for some, death."

Perhaps that's acknowledgment enough for the third platoon. It says something real and says it gracefully, even if it misses the full resonance of what happened, the elusive personal dimension of it, the private griefs and regrets. At least, the regimental history tries to look directly at the subject and describe what it sees—and succeeds often enough.


BERN Keaton and I met for the first time since the war on Sunday, May 7, 1995, the fiftieth anniversary of V-E Day. We had not seen each other since October 1944, since Bézange, in fact—a staggering stretch—although we had spoken once or twice on the phone over the years. (He would sometimes call to congratulate me on the publication of a new book.) In our occasional conversations we had talked about getting together, but it never happened.

Bern was in New Jersey, I was in New York. He had his life, I had mine. We seemed worlds apart. And there were always other demands and other priorities; we all know them. Then the anniversary of V-E Day approached. Bern called, and we had our usual exchange, but this time everything suddenly seemed right, and we made a date. Most urgent, I think, was the unspoken sense between us of how little time there was left—not only for us but for every ex-GI.

I found that I was tuning up before my visit—for we had decided that I would go to New Jersey—trying to find the right pitch for the day, the reasonable tone, and adjust accordingly. I wanted to look good and sound intelligent. I had my hair cut. I chose a flattering shirt and jacket. I looked long and hard in the mirror, regretting the twenty pounds I had put on over a half-century. I made myself ready to laugh or cry, as needed. I would be a smart kid, with Bern, for an afternoon once again.

It was a good move, as it turned out. The meeting went easily, despite obvious nervousness on both our parts. We were instantly comfortable together, once we got over the physical shock of the other's aging. My waist, Bern's white hair, our comparative slowness. Bern's wound had healed well enough so that he did not limp, nor did he complain about it during the time we had together. He made it sound as though it had happened to someone else. I had to admit that Bern had kept his sharp, craggy features, his Irish good looks. About myself, I wasn't so sure, but it didn't seem to matter once we had settled down with each other. I soon began to see Bern again as he was at eighteen and I hope he was able to see me in the same way.

We spent eight hours together that Sunday, from lunch, which we shared alone, through the long spring afternoon, then on into the evening through dinner with Bern's children and grandchildren, all of whom turned out to have more than enough lightning Gaelic wit to spare—more smart kids, I thought. (Like me, Bern is a widower and lives alone; both our wives died in recent years of lung cancer.) Bern did the cooking for the two meals, as he does almost every day of his life for himself, and he is very accomplished at it.

We talked all day about C Company and Bézange, about all that, trying to confirm each other's memory of events and people. Antonovich (O Captain! Our Captain!), Francis Gallagher, Rene Archambault, Barney Barnato, Roger Johnson, Paul Willis, Rocky Hubbell, and, of course, Ira Fedderman, who, like Francis Gallagher, continues to furiously usurp my nighttime dreams.

The names ran on, so did the events. I think Bern's memory was surer than mine. It certainly helped to give me confidence in writing this book. At one point, moving on to other matters for the moment, I mentioned to him that I had just read somewhere that more than half the personnel who served in the US Armed Forces during World War II were already dead, a half-century after the war. This seemed an astonishing statistic to me, hardly possible to accept, in fact, one that somehow carried an important warning, or omen, as though history itself—Bern's history, my history—might begin to vanish with this lethal roll call. (No war is ever really over until the last veteran is dead.) Bern looked at me blankly when I gave him the news. I think he was as stunned as I was. Then we let it pass, shaking our heads.

We also talked about books. Bern is still a great reader, one of those who seem to have taken a silent pledge early in life never to be without a volume in hand, and he keeps a record—author's name, book title, date read, and, sometimes, remarks, not necessarily kind—of every book he reads. (My books are there, too.) I found this endearing. I liked its attentiveness, its collaborative sense, its sense of participation; I like to think I share all three as a reader. Then we talked about family and work and marriage, about our wives' deaths, especially that—so-called ordinary matters out of our ordinary lives, which, after all, had consumed most of the time of most of our years.

Later in the afternoon, however, we were back to the war. It was inescapable. Bézange again. Fort Benning and basic training. Orono, Maine, the great ice palace in the north. The deadly Tennessee floods. Camp Jackson. And Europe, France, Alsace, Bézange once again, irresistible, as always, the nearly forgotten scene of a horrific crime, as one of us put it at some point—never solved. It seemed to me then that the last word could never be said about Bézange or World War II—nor about anything else, for that matter.

Before I left, we spent a lot of time looking at old photos—mainly of our ASTP buddies, taken in South Carolina before we went overseas—which Bern had fastidiously arranged in an immaculate album. The photos looked as fresh as though they had been taken the day before yesterday, fresh and clear and still sharply defined—the result, I'm sure, of Bern's loving attention. We marveled at those photos, laughed a little, remembered, then corrected each other's memory. Wonderful young faces, if I may say it myself, without a sign of care on them: skinny teen-age frames, nobody over a hundred and fifty pounds, except for Ira Fedderman, who was always an exception in everything. We laughed a little about that, too, but modestly and with some restraint. We were still not entirely sure how we felt about Ira Fedderman.

I continued to examine all those smiling faces. Smart kids, yes. And naive, for sure. It was easy to tell that we wore our hearts on our sleeves then, that we still had not assumed a defensive stance when it came to our feelings. You could see our good conduct medals neatly pinned to our Eisenhower jackets, so that everybody would notice. In our bright and confident eyes there was also the gleam of adolescent fervor. (The Army understood that fervor and used it; all armies do, they depend on it.) All of this was clear evidence to me, if I needed it that afternoon, that none of us, without exception, could believe then, at the moment those photos were taken, in the idea of his own death.

Anyway, by then it was late afternoon in New Jersey, near dusk. Bern's children and grandchildren were beginning to arrive for dinner, gathering in the living room and making a lot of good-natured noise while Bern made the introductions. As I said, they were full of Bern's wit. In fact, they outshone him. Nevertheless, brilliant as they were, they were almost totally unaware of what their grandfather had survived, or how—exactly like my own two sons. Or even of the possibility that they themselves had escaped with their own lives through his survival, exactly like my two sons had through mine.

A moment later, we were laughing again in Bern's living room, as his grandchildren began to show us how smart they really were. I liked the sound of that laughter—Bern's and mine. I carried it with me when I left. It was better than sentiment, better than the sound of trumpets and drums. Maybe it meant a kind of closure—a definitive end to the accumulated weight of sadness and nostalgia that Bern and I had both carried under the pressure of a half-century of memories. So much for so long.

I would be ready to settle for that.

# A Note About the Author

*Robert Kotlowitz was raised and educated in Baltimore. A graduate of Johns Hopkins University and the Peabody Conservatory of Music, he went on to become a book and magazine editor in New York, where he served as Managing Editor of* Harper's Magazine. *His first novel,* Somewhere Else, *published in 1972, won the National Jewish Book Award and the Edward Lewis Wallant Book Award for fiction. His subsequent novels were* The Boardwalk *(1977),* Sea Changes *(1986), and* His Master's Voice *(1992).*

*Twenty-five years ago, Mr. Kotlowitz joined WNET/ Channel Thirteen in New York and became Senior Vice President and Director of Programming and Broadcasting; upon retirement in 1990, he was named Chairman of the Editorial Council and Editorial Advisor to the station. He is the father of two sons, and lives in New York City.*

# A Note on the Type

This book was set in Fairfield, the first typeface from the hand of the distinguished American artist and engraver Rudolph Ruzicka (1883–1978). In its structure Fairfield displays the sober and sane qualities of the master craftsman whose talent has long been dedicated to clarity.

Rudolph Ruzicka was born in Bohemia and came to America in 1894. He set up his own shop, devoted to wood engraving and printing, in New York in 1913. He designed and illustrated many books, and was the creator of a considerable list of individual prints—wood engravings, line engravings on copper, and aquatints.

Composed by North Market Street Graphics, Lancaster, Pennsylvania
Printed and bound by Quebecor Printing, Fairfield, Pennsylvania
Designed by Anthea Lingeman